"HE'S KILLING ME!"

At ten o'clock that morning, Theresa Saldana left her home and was about to open the door of her car when she heard a strange man's voice.

"Are you Theresa Saldana?" the rough-looking stranger said to her.

But before she could answer, the stalker, later identified as Arthur R. Jackson, pulled a five-inch knife from his bag and began stabbing the pretty young actress in her chest. Theresa fought back, but she couldn't stop him. Her life's blood was flowing out of her.

All because she never returned his phone call.

STAR
STALKERS

GEORGE MAIR

PINNACLE BOOKS
KENSINGTON PUBLISHING CORP.

*This is dedicated to my brother
Walter Schnyder and his lovely wife, Sonya*

Some Words of Thanks . . .

To my literary agent, Sandra Watt, for doing what all good literary agents know how to do and few do it as well.

To my editor, Beth Lieberman, whose guidance and skill has made it all work out the way it was supposed to finish.

To my friend and colleague, Jerry Gross, book doctor and consultant extraordinaire for his continued support and advice.

Contents

Introduction

They will send blood, body parts, hair samples, body fluids, mutilated photographs; they will follow and lurk around you everywhere you go during the day and night; they will telephone you fifty to one hundred times a day with strange and threatening messages.

They are like a viral organism that punctures your protective skin, invades your innermost life, and soon possesses your entire waking existence.

They are men and women. They are old and young. They are gay and straight. They are the obsessed who make the lives of celebrities Rebecca Schaeffer, Katarina Witt, Theresa Saldana, Sylvester Stallone, Sharon Gless, and David Letterman living nightmares— or worse.

Mary Gabriel Lewis wanted Janis Ian and wanted her bad. Mary had been stalking Ian for a long time, sending letters and notes that were more and more threatening along with pornographic pictures and, finally, a package of dog feces. Ian got a court order directing Lewis to stay away, but nobody really believed it would do any good.

Stalkers have tracked public officials, public figures, and Presidents since the early days of America, starting with Richard Lawrence who shot at President Andrew Jackson twice at point-blank range to John Wilkes Booth, Leon Czolgosz, Sirhan Sirhan, Lee Harvey Oswald, Lynette Alice Fromme, Sara Jane Moore, John Hinckley, Charles Guiteau, Carl Weiss, James Earl Ray, and Arthur Bremer.

Mark David Chapman stalked and murdered John Lennon because Lennon was "the greatest phony in history." John Hinckley, Jr., stalked and shot President Ronald Reagan to impress his other stalking target, actress Jodie Foster.

At the same time Hinckley was shooting down President Reagan, someone else invaded the Malibu home of Linda Ronstadt, tearing the place apart, shredding her sheets, and leaving a note on her pillow, "You next time."

Record producer Phil Spector is legendary for not making a move without a security guard. Prince rarely appears without his bodyguard. Elizabeth Taylor and other stars have elaborate security systems around their homes, and reporters say that among celeb-rities Olivia Newton-John, Sylvester Stallone, and Johnny Carson have extremely sophisti-cated security systems around their estates. Carson was stalked for years by a thirty-six-year-old Milwaukee man who always signed his threats, "The King of Goodness."

Eddie Murphy has set up a separate secu-rity post at the offices of his production com-pany even though it sits on the Paramount Studios lot, which is itself protected by a squadron of guards. When he appears in public, he is surrounded by a phalanx of guards.

In December 1988, two security guards were shot and killed at Universal Studios by a man who demanded to see Michael Lan-don. He was bent on murdering Landon be-cause he was convinced Landon was a Nazi. The killer, Nathan Trupp, forty-four, of New Mexico is now in prison for the murder of the guards. He couldn't have been arrested for stalking the star.

Olivia Newton-John was bedeviled by a man who thought she was a muse sent from Heaven. Police found a death list of people in the man's home. Olivia's name was among the targets, as were five others the man had already murdered.

"Stalkers range from cold-blooded killers to lovesick teens, huddled beneath an umbrella of psychological syndromes: paranoia, erotomania, manic depression and schizophrenia. To some degree, all are mentally or emotionally disturbed; many share a family history of similar illness."

— *U.S. NEWS & WORLD REPORT*

One

Many experts say times changed for celebrities with the brutal butchering of pregnant Sharon Tate, but the law didn't start taking star stalkers into account as a serious problem until Robert Bardo murdered popular TV actress Rebecca Schaeffer.

Robert Bardo was one of the hundreds of psychopaths in our society known as a celebrity stalker. As is often the case with this type of twisted mind, Rebecca was not his first stalking target.

Celebrity stalkers tend to congregate in places where there is a high concentration of celebrities such as Los Angeles, New York, and Washington, D.C. By definition, they subject their targets to odd, undesired, intensive attention that makes the target nervous, fearful, and anxious.

Their celebrity targets are movie stars, politicians, sports heroes, radio-TV personalities, artists, senators, Presidents, well-known businessmen— anybody who enjoys or endures the public identification and notoriety that marks them as a celebrity in their field.

Hundreds of thousands of average Americans are also the victims of stalkers. They find themselves being followed, called on the phone dozens of times a day, getting unwanted and disturbing mail. It is estimated that one out of every twenty Americans has been or is the victim of some kind of stalker. Many times these stalkers of ordinary citizens have had some kind of earlier relationship with their victim— often a romantic one— real or imagined.

With the stalkers of celebrities, the relationship often exists only in the stalker's head.

Noel Koch, national security expert on stalkers with International Security Management, identifies three types of typical stalkers:

1. Can't-let-go Lovers
Those who refuse to give up real relationships that have gone awry.
2. Make-believe Lovers
Those who become obsessed with a superficial relationship established through work or leisure.
3. Obsessed Star Lovers
Those who invent a completely artificial relationship with someone, usually a star, whom they have never met. This is

the star stalker and is the one most difficult to track.

As neat and orderly as Koch's categories are, the truth is that the motivation and psychological makeup of the stalker is fuzzy and refuses to adhere to such restrictive boundaries. The Obsessed Star Lover is also the Can't-let-go Lover—the lover who has been spurned and whose love is lethally transformed into revenge. Just as all of them are Make-believe Lovers.

Even the experts can't agree on exactly what turns someone into a stalker or a celebrity stalker and where the precise line is that the ardent fan crosses over to become the dangerous stalker. The question of danger is often a matter of degree. Which stalker is the lovesick, disappointed fan, and which is the calculating, twisted, coldhearted killer?

Gavin de Becker has studied stalkers and the phenomenon of stalking for some years. While there is no absolute picture he can draw of the typical stalker, there are several traits that most stalkers seem to share. Most seem to be loners without strong relationships and are mentally troubled in some way—paranoia, erotomania, schizophrenia, and so on. They have a strong need to be appreciated or recognized as somebody important and somebody of value even though they haven't been able to fill that need through the ordinary ways of career or personal achievement.

Based on reviewing thousands of letters and notes written by stalkers, de Becker sees a pattern of talk about love, murder, suicide, God, and an imagined secret connection to their stalking target.

For the ordinary person, the intrusion of a stalker into his or her life is something that the victim becomes aware of fairly soon. An average citizen's life is not as cluttered with hundreds and thousands of vaguely perceived people as a celebrity's life is.

In the case of celebrities, initial contact is lost in the mass of fan mail and phone calls that every star and public figure gets. Only when the length and volume from one fan escalates does anybody connected with the star begin to notice the stalker. Also, because contacts with the star are dealt with by a number of people— secretaries, aides, handlers, agents— the incoming information is often not coordinated until it becomes very noticeable in volume and intensity. By the time the star actually becomes aware of what's going on, it has already become serious.

Psychiatrist Dr. Park Dietz of Newport Beach, California, observes this about star stalkers:

Public figures have always been the target of this kind of behavior, but for different reasons. It was generally for money or power. Now, it's more a love-hate relationship. In our study of anonymous death threats, we found that death threats were less likely to lead to harm in the future than were love letters.

Most stalkers believe that the stars who are their targets live leisurely, privileged lives and have nothing to do but answer the letters the stalker sends. Thus, when the stalker has written many letters and doesn't get a reply, he or she becomes enraged at the star and this rage can turn into the vengeance of a scorned lover.

What compounds the problem is that what stalkers do is largely within their Constitutional rights. For a time, before the passage of so-called antistalking laws in the various states, there was nothing the police could do until the stalker actually acted on his or her illusions; until the stalker killed or attacked the celebrity who was his or her target.

Now, many states have passed antistalker laws, but these are of questionable constitutionality and are troublesome to civil libertarians. For example, how can you make it illegal for someone to write a letter? Or, to be in a public place? Even if that person writes one hundred letters or hangs around the public place for hours or days, at what point does it cross the line of enjoying one's Constitutional right to free speech and right to assembly in public and become a lethal threat?

These are questions that are not yet finally resolved and may not be for years to come.

Two

"Robert Bardo was a time bomb waiting to explode."

That was the view of one of his high school teachers. Bardo's profile is typical in many ways of today's celebrity stalker, and it is instructive to reconstruct it here based on what we know.

Robert Bardo was a loner, unable to connect with a long-term relationship. Also, like many other stalkers, he was recognized early in life as a problem, as a time bomb ticking, but *nothing* was done.

As with so many stalkers, people in his life— family, acquaintances, classmates, teachers, authorities— encountered him along the way and recognized him as a troubled and troubling young man, but nobody did anything about him. Nobody wanted to get involved. Nobody took any social responsibility.

Everybody let him career through his disheveled life until he ended up on the doorstep of Rebecca Schaeffer's Fairfax District apartment in Los Angeles to destroy her innocent life with bloody horror.

Then, somebody finally did something about Robert Bardo. In spite of antistalker laws that have become popular, but not particularly effective around the country, this is still the primary pattern: Nobody does anything serious about the stalker until he or she has destroyed, maimed, or murdered.

Bardo's life began as the result of the marriage of his Army noncommissioned officer father and a Korean woman he met while stationed at Yokota Air Force Base in Japan. It was a typical service family's life with frequent moves before anyone had time to make strong friendships at school or in the community. By the time Robert was thirteen, they had moved several times, and were living in Tucson, Arizona, along with his six other brothers and sisters.

It was here that one of his teachers recognized Robert as a troubled youth who promised to be serious trouble to society. At fourteen, he cut out and went to visit a sister who lived in Florida where she waited tables. The trip showed him a side of the world he hadn't known about before and, when he returned to Tucson, the first signs of an obsessive trait in the young man were evident.

He became intrigued by the story of a young girl in Maine who became media famous for writing a letter to Mikhail Gorbachev, the Russian leader, urging world peace. This got Samantha Smith a trip to Moscow and worldwide attention in the press. Bardo wrote her and she replied. Impulsively, he stole $140 out of his mother's purse and hopped the bus to Maine to see Samantha.

When he got there, he wandered around trying to locate the teenager and came to the attention of the local police. They picked him up and shipped him back to Arizona.

By now, he was in high school and developing into the stereotypical stalker waiting to happen. He was bright and got straight A's in his courses, but his social adjustment was nil. He did not socialize, didn't have friends, didn't hang out with anybody, and spent his time alone and introspective.

He began writing strange letters to one of his teachers at Pueblo High School on whom he focused a newly discovered obsession. Consistent with the pattern, his letters were to a female teacher and the letters spoke of death, suicide, and murder. He wrote as often as three times a day while listening to the radio, and signed them with adventurous names such as "Dirty Harry Callahan," a movie character played by Clint Eastwood; "James Bond," another movie character played by various actors including Sean Connery and Roger Moore; and, "Scarface," a gangster movie character played by Al Pacino.

At this point, the alarm bells were going off about goblins dancing in Robert's head—goblins that needed taming. School authorities warned Robert's parents that the kid was sick and needed psychiatric attention, but the parents said he was just going through growing pains.

Ironically, Robert was smarter than his parents on this matter and knew that he needed help. The school sent a form to be signed by the parents to permit counseling for Robert and on the form, Robert wrote the following to his own parents:

> Help. This house is hell. I'm going to run away again. I can't handle it anymore. Please help. Fast.

He was a bright kid who understood something was wrong inside his head that he couldn't control and was pleading for help, but his parents said no. Nobody knows why his parents responded this way. Initially, it couldn't have been the cost of psychiatric evaluation because counseling at the school was free.

Perhaps it was the long-standing prejudice against mental problems common in our society. A kid with a broken leg is rushed to the hospital, but a kid with a broken psyche is locked in his room away from the prying eyes of the neighbors.

The year 1985 was a signal year for Bardo. The school authorities finally took action when he wrote a ten-page letter to his English teacher threatening to kill himself. They got him temporarily put into a foster home, but his parents fought this and Robert was soon back home, only to be pulled out again that summer by school authorities and hospitalized for psychiatric treatment.

The doctors found Bardo an interesting case because he was such a willing patient. They had concluded from tests and interviews that he had a severe emotional handicap. Surprising to them, he was a cooperative and eager patient, taking in all the guidance and therapy they offered, as well as encouraging other patients to do the same thing. The staff was pleased with his attitude and his progress and was disappointed when his family brought him home. For Robert, it was as if his last chance at salvation was being ripped away from him. Life at home was purgatory for him compared to the hospital where he was getting better in a more pleasant atmosphere.

He became dispirited, dropped out of high school, and got a job as a janitor at Jack in the Box starting at 5 A.M. after which he would return home to sleep, watch TV, listen to records, and try to teach himself the guitar. He had descended into the equivalent of a Dantean teenager inferno—directionless, distraught, and adrift.

He lived a Puritan existence for a teenager in the 1980s dividing his time solely between work and home, avoiding involvement with alcohol, drugs, girls, or the police. In fact, Robert was still a virgin. It was an oppressively boring real life that sired an exciting fantasy life in which he was submerged in the music of U2, Bruce Springsteen, and Guns N' Roses.

By the summer of 1986 a goddess came into his solitary realm to rule over the music, the fantasy, and over her obedient love slave, Robert Bardo:

> She just came into my life at the right time, when I was sixteen. She was bright, beautiful, spunky—I was impressed with her innocence. She was like a goddess for me, an icon. I was an atheist out there. I worshiped her.

To Robert Bardo, Rebecca was the fulfillment of every dream and fantasy he had ever had about a girl. In the CBS situation comedy *My Sister Sam,* she was beautiful, smart, quick-witted, and a virgin. She was Robert Bardo's virgin.

Now came the usual initial contact with a celebrity where the mail or phone call is handled by a staffer for whom it is just one of hundreds received that week. There is a routine for processing such contacts to build goodwill with the writer or caller, but without the celebrity actually knowing anything about the contact. If successfully done, however, the writer or caller is left with the impression that he has made direct contact with the celebrity. In this case, unfortunately, it was done successfully.

Robert had seen Rebecca on television and wrote what was probably an ordinary fan letter. For the twenty-one-year-old native of Portland, Oregon, whose acting career was off to a dazzling start costarring with Pam Dawber in the CBS sitcom, it was just one of hundreds of fan letters she received.

Rebecca was an unusually vibrant and sweet woman whose stunning beauty in high school got her into modeling at fifteen. The first modeling agent she had, Nannette Troutman, said, "She had a fresh charismatic way about her and was very gorgeous, with big brown eyes, dimples, and a beautiful smile." Apparently everybody who ever met her was taken by her beauty and personality, including Robert Bardo who had become obsessed from seeing her on the screen.

What Robert got back for his fan letter— as did hundreds of others— was a sweet, hand-written postcard that revealed his letter was "the nicest, most real," she had ever received. Then, there was a hand-drawn peace symbol and a heart with the signature "Love, Rebecca," at the bottom.

Rebecca had never seen Robert's letter and had never written that postcard. Somebody working at a fan service handling her mail had sent the postcard— probably without having read Robert's letter.

Back in Arizona, an elated Robert wrote with soaring heart in his diary, "When I think about her I feel that I want to become famous and impress her." The following June [1987], he took the bus to Los Angeles and out to the Burbank studios where his beloved worked. As a love offering, he carried a huge teddy bear and a love letter for Rebecca.

Fantasy butted into reality at the studio gate when uniformed guards stopped him. Bardo was so insistent that the guards called the head of security, Jack Egger, who used to be a cop in Beverly Hills. Egger kindly and patiently explained that there was no way they could let him onto the lot, and drove Bardo back to the motel where he was staying.

Later, back in his office, Egger called the woman who handled Rebecca's public relations, Mini Webber, and they talked about this persistent young man from Arizona. In the end, they concluded he was just another adoring fan and forgot about him. The reaction of Bardo was much different. He was so flattered by the tender care Egger had taken with him that he got his hopes up that it might be a connection that would help him get to his dream love sometime in the future. Just as Bardo was leaving L.A. to go back to Arizona, he telephoned Egger to thank him for his kindness.

However, Bardo was hurt beyond belief that his goddess queen would not see him, and brooded. He finally decided she had become an arrogant bitch not deserving of his love. A month later he returned with a large knife. Rebuffed again, he returned to Arizona and his fantasy world. For the next year and a half, he focused on new targets of affection, singers Debbie Gibson and Tiffany.

His interest in Rebecca returned when he saw confirmation that she was an evil woman whose rejection of him was because of *her* character flaws and not because anything was wrong with him. In the summer of 1989, he finally had proof that she was a fallen angel not deserving of his love.

Rebecca was in a movie *Scenes from the Class Struggle in Beverly Hills,* which the publicity copywriters painted as "another weekend of shameless sexual adventure, ill-fated romance and accidental death," and in which Rebecca romped naked through a bedroom sex scene to the outrage of her former love slave from Tucson. She had become a worthless, fucking whore in the eyes of Robert Bardo.

In the scene, she has sex with Ray Sharkey, talked about "humping," and being on the Pill. Bardo was disgusted beyond anything he ever thought possible. His dream girl. His love fantasy. *His* virgin was fucking some sleazebag and talking like a common street tramp.

It was not enough that Rebecca be revealed for the slut that she was, she had to be punished for her betrayal of his love, and punished she would be.

Earlier in a visit to find Schaeffer in Los Angeles, Bardo had once wandered aimlessly through the twisted, bewildering streets that snake across the canyons and ridges of the Hollywood Hills looking for Rebecca. His only clue was a description that had been given in a Schaeffer interview in *Seventeen* magazine.

Later, spending a carefully saved $250 gleaned from his work as a Jack in the Box janitor, Robert hired a private detective to get Rebecca's home address. It was ridiculously simple, but Robert didn't know that. All the detective did was contact the California Department of Motor Vehicles and for less than $5, it supplied the address.

Subsequently, California and other states were busy considering laws that would protect this information from stalkers and others. Drivers would be able to ask the state to keep their driver's license information confidential and thereby restrict access to businesses, law enforcement, insurance companies, and credit agencies. Unfortunately this would not have kept Bardo from getting Rebecca's address. The private detective would have gotten a credit report instead and the address would have been on it.

A few day's after seeing Rebecca in the movie, Bardo quit his job. Armed with her address, a crusading determination to avenge the betrayal of his love, and, more ominously, a .357 Magnum revolver, he set out to confront her.

On the evening of July 17, 1989, Robert went to the Greyhound bus station in Tucson and boarded the bus for the trip to Los Angeles. He arrived in downtown L.A. the next morning and took a local bus to the Fairfax District where Rebecca lived near the chic clubs along Melrose Avenue and the trendy West Hollywood community.

He got off the bus and wandered the

streets of the area for a time, and Rebecca's neighbors noticed him as a stranger in a yellow shirt. They later said he was carrying a big manila folder very carefully. He would approach strangers, pull out a photograph of Rebecca and show it to them, and ask if they knew where she lived.

Irene Tishkoff twice ran into him hanging around the neighborhood market and he showed her Rebecca's picture. She "just looked at him and said, 'What?' " and kept on walking. Irene thought he looked weird. So did Debbie Kenney who also encountered Bardo twice as she moved around the neighborhood doing her errands. "It was strange seeing him twice. You think about it for a second and then go on your own way. That's what you do in L.A."

A little later, Bardo found Rebecca's street and apartment and rang the bell. Her intercom had been broken for weeks, so she came down and answered the door in person. Robert Bardo filled his eyes with the vision of this enchantress turned jezebel and wordlessly handed her the letter he had brought.

She took it and he left to get some breakfast at a nearby diner. An hour later he returned, rang the bell again, and Rebecca came out of her apartment once more to answer the ring.

When the unsuspecting Rebecca opened the security door to this stranger a second time, Bardo pointed a .357 Magnum loaded with hollow-nose bullets at her chest, pulled the trigger and ripped her torso open in a bloody statement of his frustrated revenge. Then, he turned and ran as she lay in her oozing blood on the hallway floor of her apartment building.

The sound of the shot resonated through the building and to neighbors nearby. Richard Goldman who lived across the street said he heard two screams that were so shrill and mind-penetrating that he instantly had a rush of adrenaline and felt his blood flash cold all over his body.

Kenneth Newell, another nearby resident, came running to the sounds of the screams and found Rebecca flung on her back by the force of the bullet like a discarded rag doll. "Her eyes were open and glazed over. I took her pulse and there was no beat."

Eyewitnesses saw Bardo jog nonchalantly away from the atrocity he had committed and cut down the alley near the Sweetzer Avenue apartment building. He pulled the yellow shirt off and dropped it on the ground along with his copy of *The Catcher in the Rye*—Bardo's tribute to John Lennon's killer, Mark

David Chapman—and threw the gun holster up on the building roof.

In his pocket was a postcard from Samantha Smith, with whom he had been obsessed earlier. He had written to her and she had answered with the postcard. When she was later killed in an airplane crash, Bardo was convinced he had caused it.

After he murdered Rebecca, Robert retraced his bus trip to Tucson and came to the attention of a cop who spotted him running in and out of traffic on a freeway ramp. The officer took him in charge and got him to sit down on the curb where he could talk with him. Bardo told him, "I killed her," but, being unsure what the man was talking about, the officer temporarily took him into custody on a minor traffic disruption charge, read him his rights, and asked him who it was he claimed to have killed. At that point, Bardo said he wanted a lawyer.

The Los Angeles police were soon contacted by one of Bardo's friends in Tennessee who knew of his obsession with Schaeffer and his threats to kill her. When this friend heard she had been murdered, he figured it might be Bardo and called the police in L.A.

Bardo had already confessed to killing Rebecca. When the Tucson police were able to confirm that the actress had been murdered and the L.A. police were looking for a killer matching Bardo's description, the Tucson police faxed Bardo's picture to the Los Angeles police. They showed it to Schaeffer's neighbors who identified Bardo as the man who had been hanging around the area that fatal morning. Tucson detective, Phil Mondrian, rearrested Bardo on a charge of murder.

Robert Bardo was assigned to Pima County public defender, Lorrie Lefferts, for the first hearing on the question of whether California's request that he be extradited to Los Angeles for Rebecca Schaeffer's murder be honored.

Lefferts's strategy was to get an order temporarily ruling on the request for extradition so that her client could be given a psychiatric examination to see if he understood what was happening and was mentally competent to aid in his own defense. She figured this would delay things for several months during which time she could develop a long-term trial plan.

Judge Walter Webber granted Bardo and Lefferts a ten-day delay so Lefferts could get started on her case. She accepted that and planned to come back in a day or two and ask for more time for the psychiatric examination.

Unfortunately for Ms. Lefferts's grand scheme, the Pima County district attorney went to see Judge Webber and contended the judge didn't have the authority to give Bardo and Lefferts the delay in the extradition hearing.

Webber was uncertain at this challenge and wondered if the district attorney was right.

At that point, the district attorney called the Los Angeles Police Department and told them they could have Bardo right away if they came before the judge thought and rethought too long.

At two the next morning the L.A.P.D. escorts arrived, took possession of the prisoner, and whisked him back to Los Angeles before Public Defender Lefferts had brushed her teeth and had her first coffee. Bardo's fate was now in the hands of another woman— this time a woman prosecutor, Deputy District Attorney Marcia Clark, who would later become world famous as the prosecutor of O. J. Simpson for a double murder.

When she prosecuted Bardo, Deputy District Attorney Marcia Clark listed fourteen similarities between Bardo and John Hinckley who had stalked and shot President Reagan. She insisted that Bardo was not mentally disturbed, but only a con man who wanted attention and fame by killing the popular actress. She dismissed his stories of abuse and neglect as contrivances designed to solicit sympathy and exploit his listeners. Clark believed that Bardo was never in love with Rebecca or any other celebrity, he was just looking for a luminary to murder for the publicity and Rebecca came easy because Robert found out where she lived.

His defense attorney, Stephen Galindo, made a deal in which they traded having an extensive and expensive jury trial for the promise that the state wouldn't seek the death penalty. Even so, the judge, Dino Fulgoni, gave Robert the toughest sentence he could: life in prison without possibility of parole.

Later, when Bardo was in jail and could rationally explain what went wrong with him, he said:

My mistake was dropping out of high school. I was isolated. I didn't have any friends, never had a girlfriend. I felt alienated, but I like watching movies or TV. That's when I lost my place.

I don't think I am insane. I'm just emotional. If it wasn't for my obsession, I'd be law-abiding. But Hollywood is a very seductive place. There are a lot of lonely people out there seduced by the glamour.

Dr. Park Dietz interviewed Bardo in jail and reported that Bardo admired John Lennon's assassin Mark David Chapman greatly. "As a pursuer of public figures, that is a landmark for him. He saw Chapman as similar to himself," Dietz observed.

Bardo told Dietz about hanging around Warner Brothers studio trying to see Schaeffer and missing her one time when he left briefly to get something to drink. Dietz thought that Bardo was conflicted about whether he loved or hated Schaeffer because Bardo said that, had he seen her that day, "If she was near to me, I'd have done to her what Arthur Jackson did to Theresa Saldana." Jackson stabbed Saldana ten times with a butcher knife.

Dietz testified for the defense trying to help deputy public defender Stephen Galindo prove that Bardo was mentally ill. The prosecutor accused Dietz of being nothing but a publicity-seeking psychiatrist and extracted the information that Dietz was getting $6,000 for his testimony and the Bardo case would bring him more court testimony cases.

At the end of October 1991, Robert John Bardo was sentenced. Now, he's another stalker in jail, and she is another victim in the grave.

Three

Gavin de Becker used to handle security for Liz Taylor and Richard Burton. Today he has his own firm specializing in defending celebrities such as Prince, Joan Rivers, Dolly Parton, Robert Redford, Madonna, Warren Beatty, Jane Fonda, and John Travolta against stalkers at a fee that runs $250,000 a year and up. His files list several thousand potential stalkers that he knows target celebrities.

De Becker says, "It is possible to identify between fifty thousand and one hundred thousand people who are pursuing encounters with public figures with inappropriate reasons."

He explains that most stalkers resort to weird approaches in order to communicate with their beloved target celebrities including sending love notes, gifts, telegrams, blood, body parts, hair samples, and body fluids. If this doesn't get a rise out of the star, the stalker gets angry and tries some kind of direct personal contact, and that's when de Becker steps in. He sees his role as keeping some psychopath from "making a left turn."

One of his most serious cases came with the knife attack on actress Theresa Saldana, who had played in *Raging Bull*. Saldana was assaulted by a fifty-three-year-old stalker, a Scottish drifter named Arthur Jackson, who got to her outside her apartment on the street and stabbed her ten times with a kitchen knife in November 1982.

De Becker says he is now in constant demand because of the soaring number of fan nuisance letters that have been flooding into Hollywood celebrities in the past few years. He is called in to handle security at more and more public appearances as well as events that are supposed to be private, joyous occasions such as the Michael J. Fox-Tracy Pollan wedding in 1988.

Celebrities in Hollywood and New York have long had security guards to keep away troublesome fans and, most often, the incredibly bold and brash photographers or paparazzi who make a living getting star pictures— particularly in private-life settings. But after the murder of TV star Rebecca Schaeffer, the security business got really heavy-duty.

Rod Lurie in a story on celebrity stalking for *Los Angeles Magazine* noted about the murder of TV star Rebecca Schaeffer by stalker Robert Bardo:

What has become clear, in fact, is that Schaeffer's death was not an isolated incident. It is simply the latest occurrence in what has become a new and bizarre wrinkle in the world of criminology . . . star stalkers and obsessed fans have increased dramatically— some would say, epidemically— in the 80s.

The Schaeffer murder, for example, prompted the Los Angeles Police Department to establish a "threat management unit." During its first six months, Capt. Bob Martin reports it dealt with fifty-four cases. Of these, twenty-nine involved stalkings of very well-known movie and television stars; thirteen with not quite so big stars; and five with entertainment industry executives. Some of the stalker threats were against celebrities including Debbie Gibson, Theresa Saldana, Michael J. Fox, Johnny Carson, Stephanie Zimbalist, and NBC-TV anchorwoman Kelly Lange.

In spite of it all, Barry Levine, the West Coast bureau chief for the tabloid *Star*, whose job it is to outwit celebrities' security systems, not to harm them physically, but to get another titillating story for his readers, says:

The stars can have security guards and security systems more sensitive than a bank's, but people can still buy a star map for $2 and haunt these people.

There really seems to be a rash of these things. We seem to do more stories about obsessed fans than anything else.

Dr. Park Dietz, a psychiatrist who has long studied stalkers, says that since 1968 there have been more attacks on celebrities by mentally unbalanced people than have taken place in the 175 years before that time. About this time, state and county governments began closing down mental hospitals to cut costs. People who were loosely judged not to be a danger to themselves or society were turned out on the street to swell the homeless population and to endanger the populace.

Beyond that, Dietz says it's easy for a stalker to find his or her target:

They [the stalkers] can be very clever. They call people, like agents, who they think might have the celebrity's name on file and say they are a relative who has to get hold of the celebrity immediately because of an emergency. We've even had someone get a job with the phone company to get unlisted numbers.

De Becker says that some star stalkers have even gotten jobs as bodyguards on private security details. Ironically they are supposed to shield celebrities from stalkers like themselves. In one reported instance, a stalker spent $9,000 hiring private detectives to follow the celebrity with whom he was obsessed.

There is the added exposure for show business celebrities when they have to rehearse and perform. Their work requires them to be exposed to the public in open and vulnerable situations. Actress Justine Bateman was rehearsing for a play in a Berkeley, California, theater when John Thomas Smetek just walked into the place and confronted her. Smetek was a forty-year-old Texan who had been stalking Justine for seven months and now he was finally face-to-face with his stunned idol.

Smetek had had a delusion about having an affair with Bateman in Texas seven years earlier and he still loved her and wanted her back. To prove his love for her, Smetek produced a .22-caliber pistol and vowed he was going to kill himself before her eyes if she didn't consent to come back to him and resume their love affair.

Happily for everybody involved, except Smetek, the police arrived and spent three hours talking the man down from his emotional ledge. He finally surrendered the gun and was taken into custody.

* * *

It is not only women who are the targets, a man can easily be the victim of a woman stalker.

On October 18, 1990, Elsie Wade of Santa Monica, California, who had harassed Sylvester Stallone for years was ordered by Los Angeles Superior Court judge Irving Shimer to stay away from him. Stallone testified, "I am extremely concerned that Ms. Wade may be a great danger and threat to me."

In the previous two years, she had delivered in person over two hundred cards and letters to Stallone's Malibu beach house, one letter contained a threatening reference to the assassination of John Lennon along with his photograph. Some days she put ten or more letters in Stallone's home mailbox.

According to Stallone's security man, Gary Compton, Wade would sneak up to the house sometime between eleven at night and seven in the morning and slip letters into the mailbox.

In addition to being ordered to stay at least two hundred yards away from Stallone's Malibu beach house, Ms. Wade was likewise ordered to keep away from the offices of his company, White Eagle Enterprises. The order was for only three years, and Elsie Wade is no longer under court restraint.

Not that all those trying to get at stars are obsessed fans. Ken Kercheval, star of *Dallas* several years back, got involved in a business dispute over a popcorn company with Edward Phillips, Jr. Phillips kept stalking Kercheval and found out that *Dallas* was filmed at the Lorimar Studios near Laurel Canyon and Ventura Boulevard in Studio City.

Swinging down Radford Street off Ventura Boulevard, Phillips raced his pickup truck down the street with his right foot jamming the gas pedal to the floor and grim determination set on his face. The startled, unarmed gate guards— gate monitors is probably a more accurate description— saw this madman rocketing toward them in their little gate kiosk and leapt out of harm's way as Phillips crashed his truck through the flimsy one-arm gate.

Jumping from his careening truck just before it crashed, Phillips alit with a shotgun in one hand, fired a series of blasts in the general direction of some of the buildings and, then, inexplicably set his truck on fire. His frenzy ended when he turned the shotgun on himself.

De Becker believes that the surge in assaults and threats against celebrities is due to the intense media attention now given their lives. With a technology that spreads the images and stories about a star around the world to hundreds of millions of people in seconds, millions of people feel they have some relationship or connection with the public figure— be it a movie or TV star, politician or sports hero.

Usually, these fans are adoring and friendly, says de Becker, but there are people who cannot understand or relate to the world of reality and, for them, there is a "more workable relationship in the fraudulent reality of the media."

Writing in *Los Angeles Magazine* on the subject of star stalkers, Linden Gross noted that the dimension of this problem is relatively new in our society:

> Those obsessions [of the star stalkers]— whether sparked by admiration or aversion— can prove dangerous indeed for those who inspire them. Celebrity has *always* included an element of risk, of course. Call it an occupational hazard. The stakes multiplied in the 1970s, however, after the Manson family's grotesque execution of Sharon Tate and her friends.

Four

Actress Theresa Saldana's mother called her on March 8, 1982, with exciting news for the star of the film *Defiance*. Director Martin Scorsese's assistant had called her mother from England and was trying to get in touch with her about a movie part.

The caller insisted on having both Theresa's telephone number and her address because, he'd said, the telephone lines were down in England and Mr. Scorsese might have to send her a telegram.

A moment's reflection would have raised the question if the telephone lines were down in England, how was it possible that the assistant was able to call Ms. Saldana's mother at that very moment?

However, there wasn't room for a moment's reflection in the breathless possibility of a big movie role. So, ecstatically, the mother gave Theresa's telephone number and address to the assistant.

Then, she called Theresa to tell her about the call and the news set off skyrockets of excitement for the twenty-seven-year old actress. Her husband, Fred, was about to leave for class at UCLA and shared her happiness. He left and Saldana continued floating around their apartment in anticipation of the golden call.

The happiness ended a half hour later when her agent called to warn her that some nut was trying to find her. His scam was to identify himself as Scorsese's assistant and to get relatives or friends to finger where Theresa was. The agent listened in ominous silence for a moment, and then urgently told Saldana, "Get out of the house— now!"

Panicked at the agent's reaction, Theresa fled to her next-door neighbor, Mrs. Hahn, who took her in and said she could stay there until Fred got back. Saldana immediately tried to reach Fred on the phone without success and, then called the West Hollywood Sheriff's Office. Here she encountered the first shock that stalking victims always experience— the police aren't all that concerned about the threat to one's life.

She was told patiently that they got these kinds of calls all the time and nothing usually happened. The officer told her they didn't have a force big enough to dispatch a deputy sheriff every time there was an hysterical phone call.

They had to play the odds, and if they lost, you were dead.

Theresa recalled that after hanging up she

felt embarrassed that she had bothered the busy policeman. Still, she didn't believe she was safe and stayed with Mrs. Hahn until Fred got home and they returned to their apartment together.

They talked about moving out of their apartment to a new location, but decided that they loved the place so much that they didn't want to leave it. They also thought of moving in with friends for a while, but resisted that because they didn't want the phantom assassin—which is how they thought of him at the time—controlling their lives.

Still, Saldana was on her guard and became very careful and watchful, with Fred walking her to and from her car, classmates at school keeping an eye on her, and school authorities alerted not to give out any information about her. After a few days of nothing, they assumed the danger had passed.

At ten o'clock that morning, Theresa remembered gathering her books, kissing Fred goodbye and walking to her car. As she was about to open the car door, she heard a man's voice say, "Are you Theresa Saldana?" She turned and saw a man.

Somehow sensing this was the caller, she started to run. But Jackson was too quick and grabbed her. He took out a five-inch kitchen knife out of the bag he carried and quickly plunged it into her chest.

"He's killing me! He's killing me!" she

screamed repeatedly, trying to block his lethal blows and kick him at the same time.

But the crazed Jackson kept on with his bloody attack until Jeffrey Allan Fenn, a local delivery man, ran over and pulled him off Saldana.

Theresa stumbled over to her apartment building, begging for help, but none of her neighbors came out. Fred rushed to her side and brought her inside.

In their apartment, Fred gently eased Theresa to the floor while another neighbor tried to give her CPR and the paramedics were summoned. When they finally arrived, they cleared everybody out except for Fred, put an oxygen mask over Saldana's face, and loaded her into the ambulance.

They cut her clothing off and probed for wounds while they reported by radio to a doctor at Cedars-Sinai. Fortunately for Theresa, this was a unit equipped with a trauma suit. They pulled these plastic pressure pants on her as they raced through the city streets to the hospital on Beverly Boulevard and, once they had them secure, the paramedics inflated them, forcing the blood in her legs up into her torso and her vital organs, where it was desperately needed.

On the frantic trip to the hospital, Theresa remembered the siren and the lurching as the ambulance zigzagged through traffic, along with the crackling radio transmissions as her condition was reported to the waiting physicians. Even so, her heart stopped beating in the ambulance en route to the hospital and she had to be resuscitated.

When they arrived, her gurney was swung out of the vehicle and pushed rapidly through the emergency entrance of the hospital. She was conscious of people repeatedly shouting "Code Blue," while doctors and nurses descended on her to work on different parts of her body at the same time: one worked on her chest, another on her leg, and one on each arm. She would later learn "Code Blue" meant the patient was on the verge of death.

At the hospital they did four-and-a-half hours of heart-lung surgery and sewed her up with more than one thousand stitches to save her life.

"When I saw the surgeon, I stared into his eyes and said, 'I'm an actress. Please be careful with the scars.' He promised me he would do his best.

"Then the anesthetist said, 'You're going to sleep now,' and suddenly the pain ended and I drifted away."

After Saldana came out of the operation and regained consciousness, Fred was there by her side to comfort her, and Detective Kalas of the Los Angeles Sheriff's Department came in for a brief visit to get some details from her about the assault. He told Saldana that her stalker/attacker had been obsessed with her for a long time and had been tracking her ever since he had seen her in the movies. He was a Scottish drifter, Arthur Richard Jackson, who had been stalking her and believed that the only way he could have her as his own was to kill her and, then, kill himself so they would be united in paradise.

Kalas said that Jackson kept a diary in a tiny, tortured kind of scroll in which he detailed all of his perceptions and plans for Theresa and himself.

Jackson told deputy sheriffs that he was "the benevolent angel of death with the divine mission of killing Saldana" so that the two of them could spend eternity in Heaven together.

Jackson labeled his diary, "Death Petition," in which he mentioned Saldana fifty times.

Soon after Kalas's visit, Theresa's parents arrived. Her diminutive mother, Divina, was saddened and depressed beyond belief because of the role she inadvertently played in the attack on her beloved daughter, and her father, Tony, continued as the quiet, attentive support he had always been for the family.

What rarely is focused on is the impact of the star stalker on the star *after* an attack and on the star's family. In her 1986 book, *Beyond Survival* (Bantam Books), Saldana tells of the trauma following the assault. She was terrified of being left alone from that time forward and, even today, years later, is apprehensive about being alone.

Jackson is still in prison, but has vowed to murder Saldana when he is released. On January 8, 1991, he was sentenced to five years and eight months more in prison for sending Saldana threatening letters.

A few days after the attack and the life-saving surgery, Theresa saw the two men involved in the attack: the one who tried to kill her and the one who saved her life.

She saw Jeff Fenn, a Sparkletts water deliveryman, who had the courage to jump in and subdue a nut with a knife which allowed Theresa to get away. They had an emotional reunion at the hospital.

Then, in her wheelchair with her arm in traction, Theresa had to attend the preliminary hearing on what to do with Jackson. The police escorted her and Fred to and from the courtroom. When the judge asked her to identify her attacker, she forced herself to look at the man and point him out to the judge.

She then began a long recuperation at the Motion Picture and TV Fund Hospital in Calabasas with attention to both physical and emotional healing. It was here that Theresa conceived of forming Victims For Victims—

an organization where victims of violence help each other through the difficult healing.

Saldana is still living in terror of when Jackson will get out. Even the law passed by the California State Senate that would keep prisoners who are a threat to others in prison beyond the end of their sentence can't help her because of a twist that exempts Jackson.

As she waits, Saldana, who has since become a mother, says, "It's a very dangerous situation, not only for myself but for my family. The way I deal with it emotionally is to compartmentalize it. I don't dwell on it. If I did, I'm sure that my life would fall apart. It's too frightening and too real."

Five

You are a total shit for marrying Tracy! Divorce Tracy or you are dead! I am coming after you with a gun and I'm going to kill you if you don't divorce Tracy immediately.

— Your #1 Fan

The stalking of Michael J. Fox by Tina Marie Ledbetter was intense with her writing the star more than five thousand letters and occasionally sending him boxes of rabbit droppings.

Tina, who began stalking Michael in 1987, filled her letters to him with lots of exclamation points and expletives, but rarely her signature. Her room at the family home in Camarillo, California, was a shrine to Michael, bedecked with posters, photos, and other Michael J. Fox artifacts. When she was home, Tina played videotapes of his *Family Ties* TV programs constantly.

She became extremely upset at the news that he had changed girlfriends. He had been involved with actress Nancy McKeon, but they broke up and he started dating actress Tracy Pollan. Tina did not approve and her letters began demanding that he dump Tracy and go back to Nancy. In time, these demands began to get more and more threatening and violent.

Tina Marie Ledbetter, a twenty-six-year-old shipping clerk from Westlake Village, California, then began sending Fox numerous death threats. She sent him eight hundred alone in the month of July 1988 when he was set to marry Tracy Pollan.

Tracy got involved with Michael about a year after she played his girlfriend on *Family Ties,* where he went on to win three Emmys for his portrayal of Alex Keaton.

Tracy had left the series and, in time, had also left her live-in boyfriend, Kevin Bacon, and Michael had also drifted away from Nancy McKeon. So, when he heard through the Hollywood grapevine that Tracy was unattached as well, he immediately made the phone call that brought them back together, but this time in real life.

They dated for several months and Michael finally proposed the day after Christmas in 1987. He was positive that she would say yes, and the main worry was how they could get married secretly and settle down to some kind of seminormal life together.

They decided on July 16, 1988, as the date. The word naturally got out about the engagement and the wedding plans, and in February Michael took off for a location shoot in Thailand while Tracy stayed in Los Angeles. As it happened Tracy got the first letters to arrive from Tina that threatened Michael with violence and death because she felt he had "betrayed" her by deciding to marry Tracy. Scores of letters arrived every day and twice Tina sent boxes of rabbit manure in 1989.

On his return from location, Michael shared Tracy's concern over the threats. They both were more determined than ever to have their wedding in private. They hit upon the perfect plan. They would have the wedding in a place nobody else would ever even think of. That way, they could be happy and safe and have some special time to themselves.

Their secret plan was to get married at the serene and remote West Mountain Inn in Arlington, Vermont. To insure their privacy, a thirty-six-page operations manual was written spelling out every move of everybody connected with the wedding.

The place they had picked was far away from Hollywood, assuring it would be private. That was *before* the choppers buzzed the place.

Michael and his bride were getting ready

for the wedding when helicopters filled with frenzied photographers, hanging out on all sides, skimmed over the Vermont forest to get exclusive photos of the lovers.

For Michael and Tracy, most of their concern was actually the crazy young woman who had forced her way into their lives and smothered them with over 5,500 letters during that year.

The intense press attention coupled with the virulent threats constantly penetrating their lives predictably had an intense impact on Tracy's and Michael's existence. Michael, known throughout Hollywood as low-key and relaxed, now had to be constantly aware of security.

He accepted this as part of being a star, but even so it didn't make life as pleasant as it should have been:

> I think it's just a sign of the times. After Rebecca Schaeffer was killed, people said, "Aren't you frightened? Doesn't that scare you?" Of course it scares me. It should scare everybody. But, I'm not a lunatic about it. We lock the doors like everybody else. But, who wants to live in a cocoon? It's key that you live as normal a life as possible. I don't subscribe to the

theory that you surround yourself with a phalanx of meat and guns.

Michael did get protectively edgy after Tracy became pregnant even though he had temporarily mellowed out on that, too.

People who don't know you from Adam come up and put their hands on your wife's stomach. I was like, "Hey, what are you doing?"

At first it bothers you, but when you think about it, it's actually pretty sweet. What excites people about having babies is that it's so optimistic— it's renewal, it's everything that's good in life."

Underlying this serenity and enthusiasm were the constant threats from Tina, now coming dozens of times a day, promising to murder Tracy and to slaughter their unborn child.

Sam Michael Fox was born on May 31, 1989, unaware that the woman who had been stalking his father was now also stalking him, too.

The rabbit droppings proved Tina's undoing because she had sent them via United Parcel Service and had used shipping labels that could be traced back to her. The police tracked the labels and nabbed Tina.

Tina was arrested in May 1989, charged with five counts of making terrorist threats— which is a crime although stalking is not. At her Superior Court arraignment in mid-July, Fox testified that he feared for his own safety and that of his family after receiving hundreds of threatening letters from Tina over the previous year. Ms. Ledbetter pled not guilty and was ordered to jail at the Sybil Brand Institute For Women without bail, pending evaluation by two court psychiatrists. She was ordered to return to court August 18.

She actually returned to court September 30 and repeated her not guilty plea and was ordered to stand trial October 12.

The problem that faced Los Angeles assistant district attorney Susan Gruber in prosecuting Tina was that Tina *wasn't* nuts. If Gruber could prove Tina was crazy, she could get the court to put Tina in a mental hospital and get her out of circulation.

In 1989 in California there was no law against a *sane* person harassing a star, but not actually doing physical harm. That would have to wait a couple of years until California passed its antistalking law.

Gruber pored through the penal code searching, groping, digging for *something* with which to charge the exuberant fan, Tina Ledbetter. Finally, Susan Gruber dug out a little known statute— Penal Code Section 422— which makes it a crime to make "terrorist" threats. The test of a terrorist threat was, did it make the targeted person honestly fearful for their own safety or that of a loved one.

Michael J. Fox quickly agreed that he would testify that it honestly made him fear for the life and safety of himself, his new wife, and, most particularly, their newborn child.

Faced with that, Tina's lawyer convinced her she would be better off to cut a deal which she did. She pled guilty and was sentenced to ten months in jail, which she had already served while awaiting trial; three years' probation, which is now up; and, agreeing to obey a restraining order to stay away from Michael and his family. So far, a relatively happy ending to at least this stalker case.

Six

Dr. Park Dietz hangs his psychiatric shingle in Newport Beach, but that's not where he lives most of the time. For much of his waking hours, the doctor lives in the satanic side of the human mind; an explorer into the dark recesses we would prefer not to admit exist inside all of us.

The doctor spends a lot of time sitting in cells and talking with people like the late Jeffrey Dahmer and John Hinckley, Jr.

FBI Agent Ron Hazelwood has known Dietz for some time and has the highest respect for his ability, whatever the cost:

> His strengths are his intelligence and his common sense. I frequently find that the two don't go hand in hand. He has this ability to speak to different types of groups— mental-health groups, a jury, a police officer— and he's able to relate to all levels.
>
> I might ask one psychiatrist to tell me something about a killer and he might

say, "Well, he's an insomniac." And, he'll maybe give you some medical jargon. Park will say, "He's nocturnal and you will find him at places that are only open at night." He tells you something in a way that you can use.

In Dietz's judgment, there are at least some five million nuts or psychopaths loose in the country right now. The doctor believes some five percent of the national workforce is "clinically depressed."

In the Post Office incidents that have erupted around the country, Dietz says the postal employees and, incidentally, the employees of many private companies are potential stalkers and incendiary personalities.

Because of what he knows, Dr. Dietz is very careful to protect himself and his family as best he can. He insists that he and his wife be crack pistol shots so that they can defend themselves if necessary. The family members, including their son, practice surveying crowds of people when they are in public to see if they can discern who might be the wacko on the loose. Dietz keeps his personal life confidential, has a high level of security where he works, and prefers to remain in the background advising the police rather than being too public about his work.

* * *

The first major case where he appeared as an expert elevated him to being a superstar criminal psychiatrist. Ironically, his side lost. He was brought in by the federal government to testify at the trial of John Hinckley, Jr.

As a prosecution witness, Dietz testified that Hinckley knew exactly what he was doing, was sane, and was responsible for his acts when he shot President Ronald Reagan and three other people outside the Washington Hilton Hotel. However, the jury came back and said Hinckley was innocent by reason of insanity.

In the famous second Betty Broderick trial in San Diego where the scorned divorcée stalked her husband and his new, young wife, Dietz was a witness for the prosecution again. The stalking ended one Sunday morning when she invaded their bedroom and shot them both in bed. She killed Linda Broderick instantly and left Dan Broderick to literally drown in his own blood. Dietz declared that Betty Broderick was sane, competent, and knew exactly what she was doing at the moment she pulled the trigger. Again, the jury disagreed and convicted Betty of a lesser charge.

Dietz is a resource person for Gavin de Becker, who is in the business of protecting stars and public figures from stalkers. De Becker relies on him for his psychological profiles and court testimony in de Becker's endless fight to protect his rich and famous celebrity clients from stalkers. Curiously, Dietz won't deal with stars and celebrities directly because he finds them stupid.

First of all, they don't recognize that as stars they cannot lead normal lives. Their very stardom invites intruders, fans, and lethal stalkers. Stars are somewhat childish. They want protection, but they also love wallowing in the nectar of their fans' adoration.

Second, Dietz hasn't the patience to deal with the infantile temperament and personality of stars who are willing to pay big bucks for important security advice which they consistently ignore. So, Dietz deals with security people like de Becker, who are willing to endure the bull and baloney of the star class.

Seven

He was a sexually twisted man with an odd name: Nau.

For Sheena Easton and Olivia Newton-John, Ralph Nau is a creature in a Stephen King movie. Nau is an archetypal star stalker born on July 1, 1955, in southeastern Wisconsin to a prosperous farmer, Delmar Nau.

Nau, his older sister, Lorrie, and younger brother, Kerry, all slept on the second floor of the family home which was heated by an open grate that let the children have a clear view of adult private parties.

Cissie Nau, Ralph's sister-in-law who married Kerry, undertook being the family's public spokeswoman and became the focus of each family member's secrets. Her husband and in-laws would tell Cissie things that they wouldn't share with each other. However, no matter what his daughter-in-law said, Delmar steadfastly denied everything, to which Cissie replied:

My husband is quite a bit younger. He was just neglected, but Ralph and his sister say they were abused. Delmar was the instigator of everything that went on. His wife didn't like it. She just went along.

At age sixteen, Nau began writing fan letters to Cher and hunting in the woods to kill small animals, mutilate them, and bury them on the farm. His ultimate stalking targets became Sheena Easton and Olivia Newton-John, whom he stalked for over ten years including twice following her to Australia.

He became convinced in 1980 that Olivia Newton-John was insanely in love with him and that all her records and films were secretly romantic messages to him. He got the money and traveled to connect with Newton-John in Australia and, when his attention was later distracted by Sheena Easton who he "knew" was desperate for him to live with her, he traveled to Scotland in search of her.

Still, his focus remained on Newton-John and from 1980 to 1984, he wrote her hundreds and hundreds of weird threatening letters. He was clearly deranged and inclined to violence and killed a dog during this period claiming the dog was part of a conspiracy to keep him from being united with his true love, Olivia.

* * *

Nau was a quiet, normal-appearing student at Central High School in Paddock Lake, Wisconsin, achieving average grades and graduating with his class in 1974. A year later, he expanded his sexual and geographic horizons. He signed up for a club that allowed members to write letters to sexy women.

Unfortunately for Nau and thousands of other lonely people— mostly men— there are hustlers everywhere taking advantage of heartsick men, who are driven by the need for acceptance and love from a woman. Some of these hustlers offer expensive 900 numbers and incite them with sexy print or TV advertisements showing luscious, loose, loving women ready and anxious to talk with them. In fact, many of the women hired to "man" these phones are unattractive, having only throaty voices and enticing personalities.

Nau didn't go for the phone sex, but he did buy into the mail-sex racket with this club. Before long, he was writing long and passionate letters to a regular pen pal, Cindy, after spending the day working on the farm. He would often send along money because Cindy was always talking about needing more cash.

This postal passion continued for several years until 1980 when Nau couldn't contain himself anymore and set out in search of the real-life Cindy, who wrote him those luscious letters. Her address was in Peoria and he traveled there with $1,300 borrowed from his father.

When Nau got to Peoria, he learned Cindy didn't actually live there. Her address turned out to be a mail drop and the people there told him that they simply sent all the mail they got to an address in Arizona. He went to Arizona and found another mail drop. This time, it was a dead end because the people wouldn't tell him where the next stop was for his letters.

Nau wandered around Arizona aimlessly for a time, and it was during this phase that some vision apparently came to him in the form of Maria. Maria was a fictitious character the mail-sex service had invented, and whenever one of its members got too tacky in his letters, "Maria" would write him a stern letter upbraiding him and warning that she was prepared to discipline him by cutting him off from any more correspondence with the service. This little sham was necessary to keep the postal inspectors off the mail-sex hustler's back about pornographic material going through the mail.

Maria was the stern disciplinarian in the mail-sex part of Nau's life. It was a vision or belief as embodied by Maria that Nau claims came to him while he roamed around the mesas and deserts. Maria told Nau, as he would later explain it, to forget his mail-sex relationship with Cindy and go after Cher and Olivia Newton-John. These two women love you, need you, and have to have you!

It wasn't long before Nau appeared in L.A. in search of Cher and Olivia. He sent them letters, and when he didn't get answers, he knew it was Maria's fine, manipulative hand that was turning these two stars against him. His letters to Newton-John often made references to Maria and how she was thwarting their romance and how Ralph wanted to get her out of his life. Nau began to focus on Newton-John with three to five letters every day.

To support himself, Nau, who was now twenty-six got a job at The Cat and Dog Hospital. This brought in $125 a week with room and board at the hospital. This was also convenient for the owners of the veterinary facility because Ralph was there all the time watching after things. Dr. Ralph Goodman, his boss, spoke highly of him as a dependable employee who did a good job, and even adopted one of the unclaimed dogs. Nau named him Sam after an Olivia Newton-John song.

The people at work were aware of Nau's Olivia Newton-John obsession because his room was plastered with her pictures and posters, and she was all he could talk about during the day to the rest of them. At night, he wrote her letters.

He fixated on a sick puppy that was in the

hospital and decided the dog was really the disciplinarian, Maria, come to punish him by keeping him away from Olivia. He surreptitiously killed the animal by forcing it to take an overdose of sleeping pills. The next letter he sent to Olivia had the dog's teeth in it.

Maria's spell may have been successful because Nau began to shift his obsession to Sheena Easton. He attended an Easton concert at the universal Amphitheater in early 1982 not too far from where he worked and was specific about getting row 15 seat 8 which had a mystical significance to him that he couldn't quite explain to anybody else.

At the concert, his obsession with Sheena filled his mind with racing thoughts and he felt a swooning sensation at the sight and sound of her. Caught up in the excitement of the time, he tried to get up onto the stage, but security guards stopped him.

Foiled at getting to Sheena, he vented his frustration in his next letter to Olivia. In his mind, it was that evil Maria at work again keeping him and the woman who loved him apart. He wrote:

I truly wish I were dead and it would be so easy for me to kill myself if someone didn't do it for me and I really don't care if they did. I know the name of this

**game. It's either we go or Maria. Either
we die or she and a whole lot more do.**

What Nau didn't know was that Olivia,
Sheena, and Cher rarely saw his hundreds of
letters to them. In fact, the one person who
knew more about him and what he was writing was a man Nau never heard of or even
knew existed. His name is Gavin de Becker,
who makes his living out of keeping people
like Olivia, Sheena, and Cher protected from
strangers like Nau.

De Becker uses a bodyguard technique similar to that used by Manhattan private eye, Joe
Mullen. It is preventive protection instead of
reactive protection. Safety is not assured by hiring bodyguards. Even the U.S. Secret Service
admits it cannot protect a President from an
assassin who is willing to die in killing his target.

With preventive protection, the objective is
to be proactive and keep the unwanted assault from happening. Joe Mullen is a pio-
neer in this technique and is used by major
attorneys for their clients and Fortune 500
companies for their executives. Joe learned
the business from his father, and Joe's five
children are each private detectives, too.

Of the five children, Tom, who is a giant
of a man, is the one who loves to work the
street and applies the preventive protection

with relish. For example, if someone is stalking their client, Tom sets out to stalk the stalker. He waits for him to leave his apartment in the morning and openly follows him everywhere all-day long. Tom is visibly right behind him on the street, sitting at the next table during lunch, in the elevator with the stalker, and in the car in the next lane at the stop sign alongside the stalker.

Tom talks to the stalker out loud about the client continually. "We're not thinking of calling Susan today, are we?" "We're not going to try to visit Susan, are we?" "I sure wouldn't want to find you writing letters to Susan anymore." Tom follows him home and then telephones him, "Are we tucked in for the night with a cup of cocoa and the television? I hope so because I'll be out here all night waiting for you in the morning so we can have another play-day together. Night-night."

This does not always work with the criminally insane, but it has an amazing effect because the stalker is turned into a stalking victim and he *doesn't like it*. He becomes terrified that he will be assaulted by Tom or whoever else is out there or behind him or alongside him.

De Becker uses a similar procedure, and he also contacts family members and friends of the stalker to enlist them in controlling the stalker or to help him keep tabs on the stalker. Their motive in helping, as de Becker explains it to them, is to keep their son or friend out of prison or from being killed by security guards of the star.

De Becker started on the Nau case in 1980 without knowing it, as Nau was writing letters by the bushel to Cher, carrying a return address of "Xanadu" which was the title of one of Newton-John's movies and signing them, "Shawn Newton-John."

De Becker made the connection when Olivia Newton-John hired him in 1981 to protect her from a man who had been writing her nonstop for several years. She gave de Becker the letters Nau had been sending her, and, *click,* he and his staff immediately connected the language, handwriting, and syntax with the ones written to Cher. The difference with the Olivia Newton-John letters was that Nau often signed his real name and address.

From then on, de Becker operatives were on Nau's tail everywhere he went whether he knew it or not. They were sitting next to him at concerts and in restaurants. They tracked him everywhere and logged the places he frequented, where he worked, the people he talked to— everything. Soon de Becker probably knew more about Ralph Nau's daily routine and life than Ralph Nau did.

They had scores of photos of him taken discreetly and they had dozens of interviews with people he had been seen talking to or associating with, and yet they couldn't do anything legally about his stalking. The fact that he had a job and was regarded as a good employee made it particularly difficult.

The disturbing stalking continued in person when possible and through the daily mail to both Sheena Easton and Olivia Newton-John. In a February 1983 letter to Sheena, Nau explained that he knew why the security guards had stopped him every time he tried to run on the stage during one of her concerts. He was sure that the performer on stage was a double for Sheena and *not* the *real* Sheena because *his* Sheena would have welcomed him with open arms. Nau told Sheena that he was wise to this trick and wrote:

> They found themselves an impostor for you, too, Sheena. If that's true then she better crawl back in her hole with that other one and stay there, to put it mildly.

And more frightening to Newton-John in May of that year, Nau raised the specter of death again:

> So it looks like you got me. But it looks like I got you also because if I don't find

Olivia I'm as good as dead and if I die
I would hate to see what happens to you.

Nau's living and working arrangement came
to a sudden halt later that year when the pet
hospital was sold and the new owners had their
own staff and their own plans, neither of
which included him. With time on his hands,
passion in his heart, and some money in his
pocket, Nau went down to Los Angeles International Airport to get on a Quantas flight to
see his beloved Olivia in Australia.

He was disappointed twice during the short
time he remained in Australia. First, he was disappointed that the love of his life was not at the
airport to meet him. Second, he was disappointed that he couldn't find her even though
he spent days poking around the countryside in
the Sydney area. Dejected and rejected, he got
on a plane back to the States and his parents'
place in Wisconsin. It was May 1984.

When he got home, everybody was caught
up in getting ready for the wedding of his
brother, Kerry, to Cissie. By this time, de
Becker was on a talking basis with Nau's father,
Delmar, and they had had two significant conversations in which de Becker urged Delmar
to get professional psychiatric help for his son
before Ralph did something tragic. Delmar

either didn't want to do that or couldn't do that because Ralph held the family hostage to their fears of him and his erratic behavior.

During the year that he stayed at his father's farm, Nau would suddenly scream without cause or warning and would often crawl through family members' bedroom windows in the middle of the night, scaring the bejesus out of everybody. When a cow died of natural causes on the farm, Nau gutted it and slept the night curled up in the fetal position inside the carcass.

The whole family was intimidated and frightened silly of Nau and what he might do. Most of them thought he was a bit odd, and some were secretly sure he was insane, but they were afraid to say anything or, worse, to do anything that might provoke him into doing something unpredictable and unpleasant.

A dangerous face-off between Nau and his father came when he wanted to go back to Australia to look for Olivia again. Nobody objected. They were glad to see him get out of their lives and lower the tension level of daily life. The problem was that Nau wanted his father to put up the money. He refused.

Now Nau was confronted with his own father standing between him and his cherished Olivia. Nau pointed one of the family rifles at his father and demanded money. To his father's credit, he refused and the two men remained facing each other for some two hours. Finally, a compromise was reached and Nau was off to Australia once more. It was January 1984.

This time he not only couldn't find Olivia, he couldn't find the biggest city in Australia, Sydney. Apparently from the airport he got twisted around and ended up in the Great Outbook— that endless semiarid brushwood-covered plain reaching to the horizon in all four directions. His error was akin to somebody landing at Chicago's O'Hare airport and ending up in West Texas.

After meandering around for some weeks, Nau finally blundered into the locale of Townsville where the Red Cross contacted his father and got him a ticket back to Milwaukee— again without his seeing the object of his love and his stalking, Olivia.

The family situation changed for Nau in Milwaukee. His parents divorced and his mother married a man with two children. Nau moved with her to her husband's Illinois chicken farm.

One of his new siblings had been deeply affected by the sudden death of his mother from a stroke and hadn't spoken a word in two years when Nau and Shirley came into his life.

The boy would want to pull at, cuddle with,

and generally be all over people whom he liked just like a frisky puppy— and that would sometimes be annoying. One night when Nau wanted to watch TV, he kept pestering him and Nau pushed him out of the room and closed the door. This incensed the boy's father and he told Nau off and said that his son Dennis could go and be wherever he wanted to go and be in his house. Nau took the tongue-lashing without a word or a show of emotion.

Several hours later, soon after the boy had been put to bed by Shirley, Nau came into the family room where most of the adults were gathered and announced that the boy was missing. Nau said he had heard him crying and when he went into the child's room to see what was wrong, it was empty.

Instantly, the father was at the phone calling the sheriff and then outside searching. When Officer Chester Iwan arrived from the Lake County Sheriff's Department, he talked to everybody and decided he wanted to take Nau back to the sheriff's office for further questioning.

What triggered that was Nau telling Iwan that he had a dream about the boy and his dead mother in which the dead mother had told him that she missed her son and wanted him to be with her. At the sheriff's office, Nau told about his trips to Australia in search of Olivia and fantasized about being with her. When Iwan turned the talk over to the missing child, Ralph would only say that "A couple weeks ago my dog was killed by a truck. I buried it, but the other day I opened up the egg cooler and the dog was there."

That set off alarm bells in Iwan's mind and he pressed Nau to tell him more. When he told Iwan that he had buried the dead dog near a tree in the cornfield on the farm, Iwan immediately radioed his colleagues who were still searching. Within a few minutes they found the boy's body with his head crushed from several heavy blows. It was buried right where Nau said he had buried the dog with a curious ritualistic pattern of blood trickles nearby showing that the body had been dragged around in a semicircle before it was buried.

The sheriff's officers questioned Nau for eleven hours straight and tried to make some kind of sense out of what he said:

I hit something with an ax. I went down to . . . [the boy's] . . . room and got him dressed, but when we got outside he wasn't human anymore . . . I got the ax by the feed bin and the shovel was out by the hole. When we got by the tree the animal tried to get away and started crying and I swung at it with the ax and hit it in the head. Then I dug a hole and buried the animal. Then, I came back in the house, scrubbed my boots and washed my clothes, and went up and watched the Olympics [on television]. After this I checked . . . [his] . . . room and saw he wasn't there, so I told the family . . . [he] . . . was gone.

To the police, that was a confession and they formally arrested Nau for the bludgeon murder of his stepbrother.

Nau's other stepbrother had two reactions to the murder. First, he wasn't angry at Nau. To the surprise of many, he took a very mature and conciliatory attitude saying that Nau was sick in the head and that he didn't understand and needed help. He said, "He's sick. How can you hate him? Maybe he really wanted [him] to be with his mom."

At the same time he was very matter-of-fact in believing that the murder was cold-blooded and premeditated:

I believe it was premeditated. Why? Because the whole incident couldn't have taken more than half an hour, from the time the family saw . . . [him] . . . last [about 9:30 in the evening] until Ralph said he was missing [about 10:00] and it was probably a half-mile round-trip. He had to walk a half-mile to the backyard, dig a hole, kill him, bury him, put the shovel in the top of a feed hopper, and go downstairs and change his clothes. It's just not possible, unless the grave was already dug.

Randall Stewart, now the U.S. attorney in northwestern Indiana, was assistant state attorney for Lake County at the time of Nau's arrest and his being charged with the murder. Matt Chancey, Randall's boss at the time, sat in on a lot of the questioning and found Nau and his family life to be very bizarre.

Representing Nau was David Brodsky, the Lake County public defender. Stewart was not happy at the way it turned out:

I was assigned the prosecution of Mr. Nau for the murder of his stepbrother. When I got the case he'd made what I viewed as a valid confession. The court ordered an examination to determine whether he was capable of understanding the charges against him and was able to assist in his own defense. Those are the guidelines in Illinois law. The doctors found him unfit, so he was remanded to the state facility for treatment.

After months of therapy that didn't seem to change the nature of Ralph Nau the stalker and alleged murderer, Nau was finally brought back into court for arraignment on the murder charge. That is, to see if there was sufficient evidence that it was reasonable to suppose Nau committed the crime and, therefore, should continue to be held in the state mental hospital until he was well enough to stand trial. If the state couldn't prove that there was reason to believe he was a murderer, and if he wasn't a danger to others and himself, the state mental hospital would then spring him loose.

At the arraignment hearing, the public defender Brodsky moved to have the confession thrown out. Since the physical evidence connecting Nau with the murder was pretty thin, the confession was the main piece of evidence on which the state was depending.

Brodsky said essentially that Nau was insane and he didn't understand his rights at the time of the confession; he didn't have a lawyer present; and the cops played upon his fantasies and twisted him around to make the confession. The judge made one of the several unusual rulings in this case. He ruled that the confession wasn't admissible, but that Nau should be held over for hearing on the murder allegation.

If Stewart couldn't prove Nau was most likely guilty, Nau would have to be released. If the court decided that Nau was probably guilty he would have to stand trial, but the basis for the judge requiring him to stand trial (i.e., the confession that was ruled inadmissible for the murder trial, but was considered by the arraignment judge) couldn't be used.

The state would have to put on its entire case at the arraignment hearing in order to get Nau to the murder hearing.

The final ruling not to charge Nau was based on the judge's decision that because there wasn't any strong physical evidence to back that up.

The public defenders on the case believed that justice was done because: (1) the confession was thrown out as inadmissible; (2) there was no physical evidence to connect Nau with the crime; and (3) the time factor: Nau couldn't have done all that needed to be done in the half hour between the boy's going to bed and Nau's appearing in the family room to announce him missing.

Fighting to keep Nau off the street, Stewart petitioned another court for a civil commitment— as opposed to the criminal commitment he had tried for and lost— on the grounds that he was a danger to himself and others:

> I really thought it was absurd to say he could just walk out the door. A different judge agreed and said the evidence, including the confession, which was admissible in a civil proceeding, showed that he was a danger.

A reporter on the case, Bruce Rubenstein wrote in the *Illinois*:

For a short time in 1984, Ralph Nau, a certified star stalker, achieved celebrity status himself. Apparently, he didn't like it. "All you reporters do is lie about me," he wrote this reporter recently.

Not true. Far from embellishing the truth about Nau, the press failed to divulge quite a bit of it. Self-censorship based on squeamishness and excused by fear of litigation seems to grip the media when confronted by a phenomenon like Nau. Everything that was printed about him when he stood accused of murder was accurate, but most of the shocking stuff was left out.

Although he almost certainly committed the crime of which he was accused, Nau will never stand trial for it. After falling through several large loopholes in the criminal justice system, he remains eligible for freedom.

The Kane County, Illinois, court ruled that Nau was mentally incompetent on May 31, 1989, and committed him to the Illinois State Mental Hospital at Elgin, where he could petition for release every sixty days.

Stewart realized that this was only a stopgap, and as his next move, he wrote to some forty celebrities that his investigation had discovered

Nau was obsessed with, too, including Madonna, Connie Chung, and Farrah Fawcett.
In the letters he said:

> We feel his release is imminent and we strongly feel he is a potential threat to you. We suggest that you contact the Elgin mental-health facility regarding his release and intended whereabouts.

This may have helped the situation because Nau's terms of confinement were changed in December 1989 when the judge read some of the letters that Nau wrote to game-show letter-turner Vanna White and *Good Morning, America* hostess Joan Lunden. In his letters to Lunden, Ralph had told her he knew she wanted him to have sex in a variety of ways with her very young children and that he was ready and willing.

The judge was so stunned by these letters that he ruled Nau was a danger to himself and to society. He changed the commitment to one of indefinite term. However, some observers think Nau may be released soon.

Once in 1990, when state's attorney Tim O'Neil appeared to protest the petition, he had to read through hundreds of Nau's letters to all kinds of public figures. Nau wrote long, strange letters at the rate of six a day every day, almost two thousand a year. These were filled with references to his own semen which he had renamed "treet," and often after a day of writing these letters, he would masturbate and spread the semen over each of the pages of the letters he had written. Then, he would mail them.

"It's all there in the letters," says O'Neil. "They document the deterioration of a man's mind. By the time I finished, I felt sorry for Ralph, but I was also convinced that he should remain in custody. Very secure custody."

As O'Neil read these twisted, tormented letters, he believed he detected Nau's confession to committing a murder in Australia where he had stalked Olivia Newton-John. There were also tales of the sadistic Maria the Sorceress and stories of dead movie celebrities who would levitate out of their graves and assume the shapes of black dogs that would prey upon the countryside.

Nau's stepbrother is sure Nau will get out sometime and when he does, he will kill again. Nau, on the other hand, is still ticked off at the distorted picture the media has painted of him.

During this period Olivia Newton-John had problems with more than Ralph Nau. Also tracking Olivia was Michael Perry, an escapee from a Louisiana mental hospital, who had been after her since 1980 when he saw her in *Xanadu*. He wrote her two letters, including one that said:

> Either the dead bodies are rising or else there is a listening device under my mother and father's house. The voices I hear tell me that you are locked up beneath this town of Lake Arthur and were really a muse who was granted everlasting life.

In addition, Perry spent hours of every week listening to Newton-John's recordings and writing letters to her.

He moved to Los Angeles and began living in the Malibu hills above Newton-John's estate where he could spy on her all the time and tried twice to break into her house to talk with her. The second time de Becker's security men nabbed him, they ran him through their MOSAIC file, and identified him as a threat to Newton-John. They promptly escorted him out of California— not necessarily a legally proper procedure, but one that no one, including the police, raised a finger against.

After returning from California, Perry made up a death list of ten people on which he listed Supreme Court Justice Sandra Day O'Connor, his mother and father, three other relatives, and Olivia Newton-John and Matt Lattanzi, Newton-John's husband.

A few days later, Perry killed all five of the relatives on his list by blasting them with a pistol directly into their faces. Two weeks later, authorities finally caught him in Washington, D.C., in a motel near the Supreme Court.

In his motel room there were six TV sets with the word "Olivia" written across the screens in red. After this arrest, he was diagnosed as a paranoid schizophrenic, but fit to stand trial. He was convicted of murder and has been on Death Row since 1985 in a cell where he has the word "Olivia" written across the wall.

Eight

He was one of the greatest and most controversial rock music stars in the world. A nobody killed him to become a "somebody."

A former security guard stepped up behind him as he walked from his limo to the entrance of his building. The young man called out, "Mr. Lennon," and then pumped five hollow-tipped bullets that are designed to rip, shred, and tear gaping holes in flesh and bone into John Lennon's back.

Mark David Chapman, now in his thirteenth year inside Attica prison, says he was obsessed by J. D. Salinger's popular story, *The Catcher in the Rye*, about Holden Caulfield, an adolescent who rejects the phoniness and hypocrisy of the adult world in favor of the innocence of childhood.

He killed Lennon, he says, because the singer-songwriter had forsaken his ideals and had become one of "the biggest phonies of our time."

Chapman has been quoted as saying, "Unless you know me and know the book, you can't understand it."

At the time of the killing, this stalker-assassin druggie was nothing. Today, he has become a celebrity appearing on *Larry King Live*, with a book out about his life and the object of emulation by other stalkers and assassins such as Robert Bardo, the star stalker who murdered TV actress Rebecca Schaeffer.

Mark David Chapman has become in a grotesque sense a celebrity in the mind of many young men, and is now the subject of a book entitled *Let Me Take You Down* by newspaper reporter Jack Jones. This led to his joining the roster of guests interviewed by Larry King— it is a roster that includes four Presidents, senators, scientists, movie stars, and a vast array of notables. Now, Mark David Chapman, the cowardly killer of John Lennon, is one of them.

Chapman told about his new book for which he spent hours being interviewed by reporter Jones.

Chapman met Jones through a prison volunteer service group. He'd talked with the group's late director expressing his desire to have someone to talk with.

> I was going through a number of years of basic isolation— no visits, except for my wife . . . and I asked to see somebody. He brought Jack Jones in. I didn't

know he was a reporter for the local paper. I kind of freaked out.

Jones promised to keep their discussions
off the record and he did. Chapman contacted Jones on the tenth anniversary of John
Lennon's death (1990), telling him he had
something to announce. Chapman had been
hounded by the press and he wanted to make
a single, simple statement.

Jones told Chapman they would have to
think it through. Chapman went back to his
cell and prayed. When the two men met the
next day, Chapman said, "Let's go with whatever you want to do."

Jones' two-part article for the *Rochester
Democrat and Chronical* was printed worldwide.
It'd favorable reception led to their doing the
book.

Like many people who commit horrendous
crimes and are put in prison, Chapman
seems to have found God or, at least, Christ.
Many would have us believe that they are not
the same people who stalked and murdered
their victims. Chapman seems to play the
question of responsibility for Lennon's murder both ways.

He says that he accepts the blame for murdering Lennon and that it was not, as some
people claim he has said, the fault of the evil

that crouches inside of all of us or the devil. Then, he immediately flips and says that he is now a normal person whereas he wasn't at the time of the killing. "On December 8, 1980, Mark David Chapman was a very confused person," said Chapman speaking of himself in the third person as if talking about a stranger. "He was literally living inside of a paperback novel— J.D. Salinger's *The Catcher in the Rye*. He was vacillating between suicide; between catching the first taxi home back to Hawaii; between killing an icon."

Chapman said he regretted having killed Lennon, but that he hadn't *really* killed him— John Lennon was just an album cover to him. Lennon was not a living human, only a cardboard cutout celebrity.

Chapman has said that when he left his hotel the morning of December 8, he knew he would never come back. He had a Beatles album with him and stopped at a book seller and bought a copy of *The Catcher in the Rye* and wrote in it, "To Holden Caulfield from Holden Caulfield, *This* is my statement."

He then walked to the Dakota at the corner of Seventy-second Street and Central Park West and mixed with the other fans hanging around waiting for a glimpse of the fabled John and Yoko. When they came out and got into a cab, Chapman almost missed them because he was reading *The Catcher in the Rye*. He did nothing at the time.

He struck up a conversation with a young female fan, Jude, who apparently hung around the Dakota frequently and was recognized by the security guards and the Lennons. After the Lennons left the building, Mark and Jude went to a place nearby and got some lunch together and talked about his home state, Hawaii.

Chapman also struck up an acquaintanceship with a photographer who stood around waiting for a chance to snap a celebrity since many of them lived in the Dakota. His name was Paul Gorish, and when Lennon emerged from the building at five P.M. on his way to a recording session, Paul pushed Mark forward urging him to ask for an autograph.

He said to step up and tell Lennon he had come all the way from Hawaii and he would like an autograph. Chapman did this nervously, and John agreed readily and scrawled, "John Lennon— 1980" on the album cover before getting into his cab with Yoko and driving off.

Ironically, Lennon, who was becoming more and more of an introspective mystic and was convinced that we would all die soon in a great atomic war, gave an interview that day to RKO Radio Network. His concerns re-

flected his belief that his son would probably
not see adulthood, but would be slaughtered
with the rest of an increasingly stupid and
aberrant humanity seemingly bent on self-de-
struction.

We're going to live or we're going to
die. If we're dead, we're going to have
to deal with that; if we're alive, we're
going to have to deal with being alive.
So worrying about whether Wall Street
or the Apocalypse is going to come in
the form of the great beast is not going
to do us any good today.

Afraid he would miss John's return to the
building as he had earlier while lunching with
Jude, Chapman hovered around the entrance
for the rest of the day and into the late evening,
skipping dinner. Finally, at eleven o'clock
when it had turned chilly and windy [accord-
ing to Mark], the Lennons returned in a limo
that slid up to the curb and the rear door
popped open.

Yoko came out and walked directly toward
the entrance of the Dakota. After a few moments' delay, John emerged and followed her
to the front door of the building.

In an instance more fateful than John Lennon would ever know, he looked right at
Chapman and their eyes met for a split second. In his head, Mark says he heard a voice

repeating, "Do it, do it, do it!" John stepped on by and Mark took five steps toward the curb; wheeled about pulling out his Charter .38-caliber pistol. As he did the voice said, "Here we go!"

Mark shouted, "Mr. Lennon," and the rock star turned to face the young man he had looked at a moment before. This time the young man was in a crouch with a two-handed grip on a pistol. Before another thought could enter John Lennon's mind, the bullets began entering his chest, back, and left arm.

John was slammed forward and down by the impact of the five bullets and managed to stumble a few steps up the entrance stairs, but it was as if he had been smashed on the back by a great fist. Some present thought he said, "I'm shot" as he went down, and others say he didn't make a sound. He was mortally wounded and his life was draining out on the sidewalk.

At the sound of the shots, Yoko leapt for the cover of the entranceway, but came back a moment later when she saw John crumpled on the ground, bleeding. She cradled his body in her arms as somebody screamed a bone-chilling cry of despair.

Mark just stood surveying the horror with the gun still in his hand and his arm hanging like limp rope by his side as he, too, went into a state of shock at what he had done.

At the same moment, the doorman, who was crying, came racing over to Chapman in a display of bravery and grabbed his arm and shook the gun out of it. It hit the pavement with a clatter and the doorman kicked it away, calling to a bystander to get it.

Patrolman Jim Moran was assigned to keep fans from crowding the entrance to the Dakota where Lauren Bacall, Leonard Bernstein, and Gilda Radner lived as well as the Lennons. He got Lennon into the backseat of his patrol car and immediately began rolling to Roosevelt Hospital where Lennon died in the emergency room shortly after arrival.

More police arrived to find the surrealistic tableau of Lennon on his way to the hospital and stunned people milling around with the doorman hovering over Chapman to insure he didn't escape. Chapman sat quietly holding his book and trying to read.

When the police searched him, Chapman had fourteen Beatles tapes and $2,000 in his pockets. By the next morning hundreds of people were milling around in front of the Dakota talking quietly and wearing T-shirts on which was printed, "John Lennon, 1940-1980, Rest in Peace."

In his interview with Larry King thirteen years later, Chapman emphasized that he didn't blame the book or its fictional character or the author for what Chapman did. And, yet, Chapman *does* blame the book, its characters, and author.

> I'm not blaming a book. I blame myself for crawling inside the book and I certainly want to say that J. D. Salinger and *The Catcher in the Rye* didn't cause me to kill John Lennon. In fact, I wrote to J.D. Salinger— I got his box number from someone— and I apologized to him for this. I feel badly about that. It's my fault. I crawled in, found my pseudoself within those pages . . .

This is the same flip-flopping irrationality that Chapman uses about his reembracing religion, God, and Christ.

> I became a Christian when I was sixteen and that lasted about a year, of genuine walking with Him. The night of the death of John Lennon, I was far from Him. I wasn't listening to Him. I wasn't reading the Bible anymore. Today, I'm different. I read the Bible, I pray and I walk with Him. He forgives me. He doesn't condone what I did and that's a very important thing. He didn't like all

the pain I caused everybody and especially John's widow, but He forgives me and He hears me and He listens to me. And He is the one all these years that has brought me out of the abyss, not medications or counseling.

Chapman explains how he can be a Christian and still murder by saying that God gave us all free will to do as we want and *only* counsels peace and love— He doesn't demand it. He notes that the first child born of Adam and Eve was Cain who was the first murderer.

Mark David Chapman, one of the most infamous star stalkers in America, has his own opinions about star stalkers.

He says it happens because the stalker has nothing inside of himself or herself and that their self-esteem is zero. They get a sense of importance by writing to a celebrity or public figure and getting a reply. Chapman did the same things before the idea of killing John Lennon came to him.

He tells of going to an art gallery just because he knew that Robert Goulet and Leslie Nielsen would be there and he wanted to be in their presence. He even had his picture taken with Goulet. He felt important to be there in the presence of these celebrities, but he felt like nothing after he left.

Author Jack Jones spent two hundred hours taping conversations with Chapman for the book *Let Me Take You Down*, and says he is an intelligent sociopath who has no moral code; he is adept at deceiving himself, and senses how other people feel about things, but not in an emotional way. Rather he reads other people's feelings in a coldly analytical way, possibly in an attempt to manipulate them.

Jones draws a comparison with another stalker David ("Son of Sam") Berkowitz, who Jones also knows from his visits to Attica prison. Many of the women Berkowitz stalked looked like his mother and were seemingly having sex in parked cars around New York. Chapman fantasized about hurting a lot of people and did it by killing someone who mattered and who was loved by millions of people.

As for Chapman's immersion in religion, Jones feels that it may or may not be true, but Jones thinks Chapman believes it is true.

The story of how Mark David Chapman came to destroy one of the giant pop icons of modern culture begins with Chapman's birth on May 10, 1955, in Fort Worth, Texas. He grew up in Georgia, and as a teenager, he was swept up in the psychedelic-drug scene of the late 1960s and early 1970s as an escape from his dysfunctional family. He managed to spend some time attending DeKalb Community College in Decatur.

For a short time at age sixteen, he embraced Christianity as a Born Again and was repelled to learn that John Lennon once proclaimed that the Beatles would become more popular than Jesus Christ. The one thing that he seemed to enjoy and to do well was to relate to other young people, and he was a highly regarded YMCA camp counselor for six summers and also worked with refugee Vietnamese boat people.

His depressed self-esteem seemed to come back to him during the late 1970s and he went to Hawaii on vacation, determined he was going to kill himself sitting in a closed car inhaling carbon monoxide. Unfortunately, it didn't work and he remained in Hawaii for the next few years.

In 1979, he married a travel agent of Japanese descent, four years older than himself and got a job in a print shop at the Castle Memorial Hospital in Honolulu. After that, he got a security guard's job at a condominium complex located right across the street from the Church of Scientology that he used to harass with anonymous phone threats.

In time, he began to focus on John Lennon, who he felt betrayed the ideals of his songs. He was only a big phony laughing at the little people of the world like Mark David Chapman. He spent most of his spare time listening to the Beatles and visiting art galleries, where he delighted in arguing with other visitors over the relative merits of various artists.

He set out on his journey to stalk and murder John Lennon. He left his wife and on October 23 quit his job as a security guard. On his last day, he was wearing his guard uniform, but with a name tag that read, "John Lennon." He signed out on the logbook for the last time as "John Lennon."

Four days later, he walked into the J & S Enterprises store and bought a Charter Arms .38-caliber pistol, which was given to him immediately since he had no police record. In the remaining time in Hawaii, he borrowed $2,500 from a credit union, and on December 6, 1980, flew to New York where he stayed at the West Side YMCA for the next two days. Then, he moved to the Sheraton Center Hotel and killed John Lennon on December 8.

At his first hearing he pled not guilty, and his lawyer Jonathan Marks planned an insanity defense. At the hearing on June 22, 1981, Chapman startled his attorney by saying he had discussed the matter with God and God had told him to admit he killed John Lennon. So, he pled guilty to second degree murder.

The following month on July 24, Chapman was sentenced to twenty years to life. He responded to the judge's sentence by reading a passage from *The Catcher in the Rye*. He is now in Attica and the chances of his ever being released are remote.

Nine

We are a nation that worships celebrities. Some say that we yearn, as a nation, for a royal family; lacking that, we have turned entertainment stars, sports figures, and a handful of politicians into royalty. Yet that doesn't explain why some people have also turned criminals or anyone who has gotten what the late Andy Warhol called his fifteen minutes of fame into celebrities.

Most of these people are not achievers of substantial merit who have been accorded public celebrity status. The Hillside Strangler and Pam Smart are more adored and better known than Jonas Salk, the inventor of the polio vaccine, or I.F. Stone, the late erudite political analyst. Both the Hillside Strangler and Pam Smart have fan clubs, receive regular offers of money and marriage, and Pam has one male admirer who sends her sexy lingerie every month.

Author and social critic Richard Schickel used the wisdom of Obi-Wan Kenobi from the movie *Star Wars* to explain it when he said, ". . . the lives of celebrities create a sort of psychic energy field that surrounds us and penetrates us, binding our universe together."

Through the imagined intimacy of television and movies, radio, tabloid newspapers, and weekly news magazines, we have become a homogenized nation with people in Nashville, Maui, Bangor, Tucson, and Nome, all experiencing the same news, the same stars, the same celebrities at the same relative moment of the day.

Once a star was someone who achieved something in a particular field. They were often only stars to a narrow group of fans and enthusiasts. This is still true to some extent. Or, they could have achieved something that everybody seemed to know about and were stars to the whole world. This might include a sports figure, such as Babe Ruth or a scientist whose work became widely known, such as Albert Einstein.

Or, they might have done something extraordinary, but evil, such as Hitler, John Dillinger and Charles Manson that did not give them fame but, rather, infamy. They emerged from out of the ordinary and in a twisted sense became celebrities.

However, there is another kind of celebrity who is the product of modern times, modern promotion, and modern media. One of the significant marks of being a celebrity today is to be in or, better yet, be on the cover of magazines such as *People, Time,* and *Cosmopolitan.* Agents and handlers finagle, fume, and fight to get their clients in magazines and, ideally, on their covers. Simply being in the magazine makes one a celebrity.

The success of *People* magazine spawned imitators of its celebrity journalism such as *Us* and *Vanity Fair* and endless personality-celebrity-centered TV shows such as *Inside Edition, American Journal, Hard Copy,* and the myriad of TV talk shows.

The creation of celebrities has also created celebrity stalkers. Richard Schickel has a concept he calls, "The Subculture of Assassination."

Schickel personifies the central figure in this Subculture of Assassination as the new kind of antihero that the English critic Alexander Walter formulated and labeled, "The Benign Betrayer." Walter describes this person—man or woman—as stuck in a life role or life situation that is never going to get significantly better for them and who decides they must change that situation in whatever way they can. In other words, if the system you're in isn't going to reward you properly, change the system to one that will reward you. One way of doing that is to pull it down by betraying embarrassing secrets in a way that makes you notorious as the betrayer.

The self-benefiting steps beyond betrayal for the Benign Betrayer, says Walter, is to (1) betray or indict yourself at the same time as you are betraying the others in the institution so you can assume the role of the repentant sinner and his biblical claim to special sympathy and, (2) claim that it was only the insistence of a "High Good" or a call from a "Higher Power" that forced the Benign Betrayer to expose his friends and colleagues.

Jack Henry Abbott wrote in such an engaging way from prison that Norman Mailer took up his cause and got him released, only to have him stab to death an innocent waiter at the Bini-Bon restaurant where Abbott and two female companions were having a celebration dinner on July 18, 1981.

In her *New Republic* article on The Subculture of Assassination, Priscilla Johnson McMillan paints the portrait of this quintessential American type: "The lone assassin, one who lacks a sense of who he is, shops among artifacts of our culture— books, movies, TV programs, song lyrics, newspaper clippings— to fashion a character."

In some ways, it comes down to each of us wanting certification that we exist and that we are somebody of value.

* * *

As we grow from infancy, we become aware of our helplessness and lack of meaning in the totality of the universe. What do we matter when we will be here only a short time and then die? Who will care? Who will remember?

For some, such unimportance is intolerable and they seek to be known, to be remembered, and to be somebody. In centuries past that meant building the Pyramids, conquering vast empires, discovering radium, trekking to the North Pole, or writing the history of Rome. Today, it's being on television since that is the most universal medium of recognition.

National Public Radio [NPR] commentator, Daniel Schorr, said some years ago that politicians and public figures spend a lot of time jumping up and down waving their hands to be recognized by the television camera. They know, he said, that unless they are on national television they don't, in fact, actually exist.

In addition, alliance with someone who already is recognized as "somebody" certifies us as "somebody too." This is why people want their pictures taken beside political leaders, entertainment stars, and famous people. It certifies that they are "somebody."

Fans seek to bond with heroes and heroines so they too, can be glamorous and famous. When the object of a fan's adoration ultimately rejects the fan, he or she is left with what the psychologists call the Rage of Abandonment and the Betrayal of Love. That's when the fan's admiration and love turns bad and becomes vengeful.

Robert Bardo fell in love with Rebecca Schaeffer and knew that he would be happy and "somebody," if only she would love him. When it became clear that she would not love him, he needed to get revenge by shooting her down in cold blood on her doorstep.

When John Hinckley, Jr., decided that if he was Jodie Foster's lover, his life would be happy and fulfilled and he would be "somebody," he decided he had to do something to impress her and win her love.

What he wrote to her was lost in the avalanche of three thousand cards and letters she received every month. He was a lost soul searching for some way to be "somebody" while drifting through life as an unanchored, bewildered nobody.

He believed that by being with Jodie Foster—being her lover, her companion, her protector—of being "somebody" because she anointed him as worthy of being her man.

Days later, after President Reagan had been shot along with his press secretary, Jim Brady, the police found another letter addressed to Jodie Foster in John Hinckley's hotel room. He explained what he was doing for her, "Jodie, I'm asking you please to look into your heart and at least give me the chance with this historic deed to gain your respect and love."

Five hours after he shot the President and was being questioned by Secret Service agents, Hinckley's question was, "Is it on TV?" He was asking of them, "Am I somebody?"

In a letter Hinckley sent to Stuart Taylor, Jr., a reporter for *The New York Times*, after he was sent to St. Elizabeth's Hospital in Washington, D.C., he spelled out his victory:

Jodie Foster may continue to outwardly ignore me for the rest of my life, but I have made an impression on that young lady that will never fade from her mind. I am with Jodie spiritually every day and every night. I have made her one of the most famous actresses in the world. Everybody, but everybody, knows about John and Jodie. We are a historical couple whether Jodie likes it or not.

At one time, Miss Foster was a star and I was an insignificant fan. Now everything is changed. I am Napoleon and she is Josephine. I am Romeo and she is Juliet. I am John Hinckley, Jr., and she is Jodie Foster. The world can't touch us. Society can't bring us down.

She will never escape me. I may be in prison and she may be making a movie in Paris or Hollywood, but Jodie and I will always be together, in life and in death . . .

John Hinckley, Jr., turned himself into "somebody."

Ten

Andrea Evans has starred in the TV daytime soap, *One Life To Live,* but a stalker won't let her have her own life to live. Today Andrea Evans lives in constant fear because of a Russian immigrant who has been stalking Andrea since 1987.

Her life seemingly went along the stardust trail that every aspiring actress dreams of following. She attended the University of Illinois studying theater, and when she finished in 1978, she set out for New York City where she landed a role on ABC's *One Life To Live* for the next three years. Then, she turned fantasy into reality when she married her co-star Wayne Massey, and left the show to live her life in the real world.

But the real world was tougher than the fictional world, and four years into their partnership, Wayne and Andrea were out of the marriage. She was so in demand that *One Life To Live* took her back immediately.

* * *

In July 1987 her parents came to visit her in New York and she tried to show them around town and bask in her success with the people who mattered most to her. One of the things her mother wanted very much to do while in Manhattan was to visit *The Morning Show* and her idol, Regis Philbin. This was easy for Andrea because she had been a guest on the show a number of times and was friends with Regis.

They went to the studio and saw the show; her mother was thrilled. After the show was off the air, Regis came out and talked with them and commented that he had gotten Andrea's letter about the dog. Andrea professed confusion because she hadn't written him a letter about a dog or about anything else. She didn't even have a dog.

Regis had an aide run up to the office and fish the letter out of the file to show Andrea. Puzzled, she glanced at the note and concluded it was somebody impersonating her and told Regis as much. Neither of them thought much about it anymore.

Another curious set of incidents struck Andrea at home. She got a series of letters with faked legal documents about a lawsuit in which she was supposedly taking Regis to court. Again, she dismissed it as a crank, but

what happened next couldn't be sloughed off
that easily.

She was in the lobby of the ABC studios
north of Lincoln Center in Manhattan some
days later having just said an affectionate
goodbye to her current boyfriend. She was
getting ready to return to the studio and
work. Suddenly a small man dressed in a
neat, tailored suit appeared from the outside,
grabbed hold of Andrea by the arm and
spun her around.

At the same time, he began screaming at
her in rage about something over a dog and
throwing what appeared to be legal papers
at her. Fortunately, the ABC security guards
were on the alert and came storming to her
aid and quickly ejected the man from the
building. They made no attempt to detain
him or call the police.

Phoning the police was left to Andrea, who
figured there must be some connection between the incidents at the Regis Philbin show,
the phony legal papers that came in the mail,
and this attack by the short man. The police
dismissed it as another crank incident and
told her to be careful, but to forget it.

The short man started to get very serious
about his stalking, and used blood to make

sure that Andrea didn't forget it the next time.

He showed up at the ABC studio again and, when told Andrea was gone, he slashed his wrists. Energized into action, the staff called 911 and got an ambulance and paramedics to the scene. The stalker was hauled away to Bellevue Hospital, where he identified Andrea as his next of kin on the paperwork.

Thus began a nightmare that would destroy the dream life Andrea had enjoyed. Against her will this Russian immigrant has become a permanent part of her life. After enduring it for the next two years, she surrendered the life she had and went into retirement. That's where she is today— planning her existence to avoid an obsessed stalker that the law can't seem to put away. In *People* magazine Evans conjured up this real-life horror:

When you know there's somebody out there who wants to kill you and you don't know where he is and he can pop up at any moment, it's sort of like this: Imagine you're alone in a dark parking lot and you hear noises and you still have to go to your car. You keep looking behind you because you think you hear somebody. Well, what if you aren't imag-

ining a person there, you know he is . . .
Every time you walk down a dark street,
you know he's there . . .

In Andrea's case, a math professor for-
merly of the Soviet Union, whose name she
doesn't know but who is known to the FBI
as having stalked Ronald Reagan and the
Secretary of State with a meat cleaver, is now
stalking her.

Whenever he gets caught by the police, the
result is the same. The doctors look at him
and pronounce him a paranoid schizophrenic
and lock him up for a couple of months
while dosing him on behavior-adjusting
medicine. They decide he's okay and let him
out. He immediately goes back to stalking
until he is arrested again and repeats the
drill with the doctors once more.

It didn't help Andrea's frame of mind to
have the FBI or the police call her every few
weeks and tell her the short Russian was
loose again and she must be very careful.

She finally took her savings, resigned from
the show, and dropped out of sight to write
a movie or book about her experience. She
is valiantly trying to make a new life with
her boyfriend; it is the first peace she has
known in a long time.

* * *

But, Andrea Evans is so popular on the show— and in her heart she's still hungry for the public's acclaim— that she let herself be talked into a visit to New York to make a few guest appearances:

I got up that morning and an ABC limo came to drive me to the show. I got out and the limo driver was walking me in. In the crowd was the stalker. I saw him. I saw his face. He chased me into the building. I ran, screaming for the guards to stop him. Unfortunately, the guards just scared him away. I left the first thing the next morning. It was pretty devastating.

Her only public appearance since then has been on *Larry King Live* on CNN where she explained to the audience how this stalker had destroyed her career and ruined her personal life:

The problem is he's mentally incompetent to stand trial, so I can't even have him imprisoned. After he learned of my stay in New York, he disappeared and got to Washington where he was threatening political figures in order to get my attention.

For a long time, it cost my desire for

a career, and that was very painful for me. For a long time, work meant possible death to me. We need federal laws. We need to put these people behind bars, so people like myself and hundreds of thousands of other people don't have to live like this.

Andrea now lives away from the spotlight, almost in hiding. It's as if *she* were the criminal, and her tormentor runs free to prey on her and, perhaps, other innocent victims, too.

Eleven

Vanna White has been stalked for a long time by Roger Davis, who most recently jumped out of the audience during a taping of *Wheel of Fortune*, wearing a camouflage outfit and dog tags, screaming that Vanna's boyfriend [now her husband] was an evil Mafia killer. Davis is positive that Vanna is destined to marry him, but Vanna and her husband don't agree and have gotten restraining orders against Davis.

Teri Garr has been stalked for five years by a woman who trespasses on her residence at least three times a day claiming she only wants to give the star a bead necklace which has been broken and put into five envelopes.

Robert Kieling, a Saskatchewan farmer, has stalked singer Anne Murray for twenty years. He called her office 235 times in 1989, in violating a court order; was convicted; sent to prison; paroled on probation; and violated probation by calling or approaching Murray at her Toronto home 128 times in two months around New Year's 1991. His reason is an obsessive delusion that the two of them have been having a torrid, secret love affair for two decades.

Kieling's legal defense was that the government was violating his constitutional right to freedom of association.

Daniel Vega was a man obsessed with several celebrities, and he possessed a stalking fixation on Donna Mills. Vega was also an escaped convict who had been serving three life sentences for kidnapping.

At the Pasadena, California, courthouse, where he was awaiting a pretrial hearing for threatening to murder the father of rock star David Lee Roth, Vega overpowered a guard at gunpoint in the holding cell, unlocked two doors, and hobbled in chains down to the parking lot where he fled in a pickup truck with two accomplices. No one had any idea how he got a gun into the courthouse holding cell.

The next morning a resident of nearby Mt. Washington on Vista Gloriosa Drive called her private security guard services after seeing a man asleep in a pickup truck in front of her house. A security guard came, knocked on the window of the truck, and was suddenly confronted by Vega pointing a pistol at his face. Vega took the guard's gun and fled; the guard immediately summoned police.

Police and dogs found Vega hiding under a house some distance away and ordered him out. He came out with weapons at the ready and officers shot and killed him on the spot.

While in prison, Vega had been trying to sell to the supermarket tabloids his story of Mafia connections and several celebrity love affairs, including the imagined one with Donna Mills. On the day of Vega's escape and the day before he died, *The Globe* published one of these describing his six-month affair with Donna Mills.

She is not a dangerous person, only a woman with the delusion that she is Mrs. David Letterman.

Margaret Ray thinks she is Mrs. Letterman and has been arrested eight times for trespassing on David Letterman's property in New Canaan, Connecticut. Ironically, she was the one who inspired the new antistalking law in Connecticut, but cannot be prosecuted under it. That's because the law requires the stalker demonstrate that he or she is a violent danger to the victim, and Margaret is not.

Ms. Ray, who says Letterman is "the dominant figure in my life," began stalking the comedian back in 1988 when she stole Letterman's $80,000 Porsche and began driving it around Connecticut with a small child in the front seat. At one toll booth, she introduced herself to the toll collector as Mrs. Letterman and the child as David, Jr.

She was, however, sentenced to six months in prison in June 1992 for breaking and entering Letterman's house. She was also arrested later for going into his unlocked garage and leaving two cookies, a bottle of whiskey, and some letters.

On May 5, Margaret, forty-one, left a letter and a book about meditation in Letterman's driveway. Alerted, the police searched the area, but could not find her. She had hitched a ride to the train station with three teenagers.

Letterman has said that he doesn't want to prosecute Ms. Ray, whose home apparently is in Crawford, Colorado, and that he just wants to be left alone. Regarding the last letter she left, Letterman didn't want to disclose the contents, only that it did not contain any threats.

Pop singer Janet Jackson has had an unpleasant turn in a charade between frightened victim, mindless stalker, and helpless legal establishment.

Frank Jones traveled to New York and then to Southern California, where he fixated on

Rebecca Schaeffer (*Phil Roach/Photoreporters, Inc.*)

Theresa Saldana (*Lisa Rose/Globe Photos, Inc.*)

Tina Marie Ledbetter (*Los Angeles Times*)

Michael J. Fox
(*Courtesy of Ron Galella*)

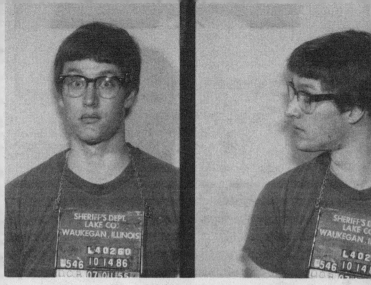

Ralph J. Nau
(By Permission of Office of Sheriff, Lake County, Illinois)

Olivia Newton-John
*(Stephen Trupp/
Globe Photos, Inc.)*

John Lennon and Yoko Ono (*Brian Hamill/Photoreporters, Inc.*)

Andrea Evans
(*Photoreporters, Inc.*)

Vanna White
(*Globe Photos, Inc.*)

Donna Mills
(*Michael Ferguson/
Globe Photos, Inc.*)

David Letterman
(Courtesy of Ron Galella)

Margaret Ray
(AP/Wide World
Photos, Inc.)

Janet Jackson (*Phil Roach/Photoreporters, Inc.*)

Sharon Gless *(Globe Photos, Inc.)*

Joni Leigh Penn *(AP/Wide World Photos, Inc.)*

Monica Seles *(Courtesy of ARD/NDR-TV/Photoreporters, Inc.)*

Günter Parche
(Photoreporters, Inc.)

Katarina Witt *(Burstein/Photoreporters, Inc.)*

Gerald Ford
*(Allan S. Adler/
Photoreporters, Inc.)*

Jodi Foster (*Globe Photos, Inc.*)

Ronald Reagan
(*Mark Reinstein/
hotoreporters, Inc.*)

Sol Wachtler *(Burstein/Photoreporters, Inc.)*

Janet Jackson. He became convinced that he
was Janet's husband and began writing her
repeatedly and then making threats against
her brothers, claiming they were keeping him
away from his wife, Janet.

He was finally arrested as he stood yelling
in the driveway of the fenced and gated Jackson compound in Encino. How he got past
the locked gates, no one seemed to know, but
once he was standing in the driveway and
started yelling, the panicky security guards
came running.

Jones was not violent, but he did make
threats against Janet and her brother Jermaine. The guards decided that he was just
a little nutty, not planning to hurt anybody,
but simply convinced that he was Janet's husband and determined to get her attention.

The police took Jones away and he was assigned a public defender. Appearing in
court, he pled not guilty to three misdemeanor trespassing counts, two for making
terrorist threats, and two for stalking. His
bail was set at a trivial $15,000, and he was
to appear in court three weeks later for trial.
The maximum penalty Jones faced was four
years in county jail and a $4,000 fine.

Frank Jones's miscalculation was to do
what he did in 1992 in California because the
murder of Rebecca Schaeffer jolted the 1990
legislature into passing an antistalking law.
The police have the right to arrest anyone

they believe has maliciously followed, harassed, and threatened someone. This landmark law is being copied by states around the country, and it triggers alarm bells with people who worry about its implications for civil liberties.

On July 12, 1993, Jones was sentenced to two years in prison for sending forty threatening letters to Janet Jackson after admitting that he had made a lot of mistakes but claimed that he could now control himself with the help of some medicine. In his letters, he told Janet that they were married and then threatened her, her boyfriend, her brothers, Jermaine and Michael, and her movie director, John Singleton.

Jones went to jail on a plea-bargain deal in which he didn't plead guilty to doing anything wrong against Janet. Rather, he pled guilty to one count of threatening her boyfriend with the agreement that all other charges would be dropped, and they were.

Her brother had been stalked by a forty-one-year-old legal secretary who called herself Billie Jean Jackson and claimed to be his wife. Violating a court order to stay away from the Jackson family compound in Encino, California, she was sent to jail for two and a half years, but promised she'd be back when released.

* * *

A variation on the ordinary stalking is what has been happening to the noted jazz soprano saxophonist David Liebman, known for his recordings *Turn It Around* and *Setting The Standard*. Liebman has been stalked since 1991 by a man who is trying to take over his identity. The stalker is out to embarrass and destroy Liebman's career by impersonating him to people in the music business.

The phony Liebman calls concert halls, says he is Liebman, and cancels concert dates. He writes insulting letters on copies of Liebman's letterhead stationery that he sends to important business people in the music industry and other distinguished musicians.

To Liebman, his impersonator sends dead fish, makes obscene phone calls, and once sent a picture of a man in a wheelchair with his eyes burned out. Liebman is confined to a wheelchair from having had polio as a child.

The police have analyzed the handwriting from the various pieces of mail and they think they know who the stalker is, but they are not yet ready to make an arrest. Liebman wishes they would, "It's difficult enough to work as a jazz musician without this garbage."

NBC-TV news anchorwoman Kelly Lange had been stalked for five years by Warren

Sevy Hudson, an infatuated fan who flooded her with phone calls, flowers, cards, gifts, and letters while telling all his friends that he and Kelly were engaged.

Hudson began his stream of love letters to Lange in 1985 when he was working as a telephone salesman and living in various motels around the Los Angeles and San Fernando Valley area. He was unnaturally infatuated with the blonde, perky newscaster, who had made her own break in television by winning a contest to be the weathergirl for KABC, a Los Angeles radio station.

She debuted on the air as "Miss Dawn" giving weather reports in the morning while her afternoon counterpart was "Miss Eve." From that, Kelly Lange was able to make the transition to television and, ultimately, the news anchor's desk at the local NBC station, KNBC.

She was admired and loved by a number of people who saw her on the air, but Hudson was obsessed with her to such a point that when his mother died he sent his mother's furs and jewels to Lange as a love offering.

Hudson put himself on the line publicly in his illusionary romance with Lange by pouring his heart out to the KNBC telephone receptionist and by telling all his friends and coworkers that the two of them were engaged to be married. He was setting himself up for an embarrassing fall.

When she failed to respond properly, he began threatening to murder her. He wrote her, "I am going to blow your head off in the parking lot some night and you are never going to know what hit you."

He got fired in August of 1990 from the telemarketing firm where he worked and told a former colleague that he was bored with life and had decided to drive over to NBC's Burbank studios and shoot Kelly. The co-worker reported him to the police and he was arrested in possession of a .38-caliber pistol at the motel room where he lived.

He was finally convicted of making a terrorist threat under a law passed three years after he started stalking Lange and was sentenced to three years in prison.

Hudson's defense attorney, James Coady, a deputy public defender tried to get the judge to agree to probation since Hudson had no previous criminal record. The judge, however, agreed with the prosecutor, Deputy District Attorney Susan Gruder, that Hudson needed the three years in prison to be sure he underwent psychiatric therapy.

The first indication of a stalker came to TV anchorwoman Jann Carl during the hot summer of 1990 when a man kept trying to get a date with her by bothering her on the phone. She refused him repeatedly and he began stalking her and following her home. He was able to send letters to her house which upset her because she didn't think anybody but a handful of friends knew where she lived.

The stalker finally tried to extort $31,000 from her in exchange for suppressing sexually explicit videotapes he claimed to have of her but which, in fact, never existed.

In 1990 in Buffalo, New York, Laurie Lisowski innocently answered a fan letter and sent along a photo. That was the beginning of her stalking by Michael G. Taylor, who had made numerous harassing and threatening phone calls to the WGRZ-TV anchorwoman.

Soon, he was calling her just as she got home or just as she arrived at work, and it was clear that he must have been following her and knew where she was much of the time.

While she was reporting on the St. Patrick's Day parade in Buffalo, somebody threw a naked Barbie doll on the hood of her news station car. This was explained a few days later in a note that said it was done because she had mentioned liking Barbie during one of her broadcasts.

He kept after her with letters and phone calls and, finally, approached her as she was outside the Channel 2 studio. "He seemed

kind of meek. He asked if I was dating someone and I said I was. He said, 'It doesn't seem
like you are. Can I go out with you?' "

He chastised her in a subsequent letter and
insisted that whenever a woman is offered love
by a man she is duty-bound to accept it. She
talked to a friend on the police force, Marty
Harrington, but she didn't want to create
trouble by filing any complaint against Taylor.

"My fear was if the police got involved,
he'd get upset and retaliate. You tell yourself
he's not dangerous, but you don't know."

Taylor started sending sexually threatening
proposals, and had written that the two were
perfect for each other since they shared the
same work schedule. He was convinced that
she was sending him secret messages during
her news broadcasts including telling him to
think about sex.

After being stalked by Taylor for three
years, Lisowski was able to have him arrested
on March 24, 1993, under a new antistalker
law that had been passed in New York state
the previous November.

The next day a court order and a warning
were issued by Judge Russell to Taylor to stay
away from Lisowski, which Taylor immediately
violated by appearing at the station with flowers and a love letter. This time Taylor was arrested for violating the court order, but the
charges were dropped on his promise to seek
psychiatric care. Taylor had been fined $100

in 1987 in Royalton Town Court for stalking another woman in the town of Newfane.

On April 17 Taylor was arrested and on the twenty-first appeared again before Judge Russell on misdemeanor aggravated harassment charges and for contempt of court in violating the March 25th Stay-Away order. Judge Russell reimposed his Stay-Away order and warned Taylor that he faced a year in jail if he violated it again.

The judge ordered vice detective Martin Harrington to arrest Taylor and directed that he be taken to Erie County Medical Center for a month-long psychological evaluation.

The evaluation concluded Taylor was not a danger to himself or to anyone else and recommended he be released. Judge Russell required Taylor to post a $5,000 bond to guarantee that he would stop harassing Lisowski.

Ironically, not all of the telephone calls and letters sent to Lisowski were from Taylor. Taylor lives in the town of Lockport and authorities say her second stalker lives in the town of Cheektowaga. Police have interviewed the Cheektowaga man and he admitted stalking Lisowski for a year or so. His identity has not been made public.

Twelve

Star stalking is a contradiction in terms. Celebrities seek out the love and adoration of fans but then are terrified when it grows out of hand and the fan becomes a lethal stalker.

One of the underlying defenses against star stalkers is for public figures and celebrities to understand the nature of the problem that threatens their lives.

With scores of talk shows, tabloid TV programs, and tabloid newspapers all chasing after titillating exposés and co-opting the so-called legitimate media into doing the same thing, stalking of stars and celebrities has become a national sport.

In fact, a lot of legitimate people are paid a lot of money to literally stalk stars and celebrities. Let's examine part of that and see how it lends respectability to the concept of star stalking.

Alan Zanger is a paid professional who earns enormous sums of money for intimate and candid pictures of celebrities. He and his colleagues are literally paid money by the Tabloids, to follow celebrities, to invade their privacy, and to expose them to the ridicule of the world.

Alan has been beaten with a baseball bat, been run off the road, and shoved countless times, but he still keeps coming back to stalk celebrities for his tabloid employers.

It used to be more civilized, but because the money is so much more today, the once polite give-and-take between the paparazzi and celebrities has evolved into confrontations, lawsuits, and restraining orders.

This kind of stalking is driven by an insatiable interest in the lives of the stars that pushes the paparazzi to go beyond the candid shot to the clandestine shot. Whether his assignment is the Madonna/Sean Penn or Fox/Pollan wedding or Fergi topless sucking her "financial adviser's" toes poolside, getting the shot is Alan's only concern.

Brian Williams, described as tenacious and imaginative and one of the *Enquirer*'s star reporters, broke the story of one actress's bizarre cancer treatments and another actress's having an affair with a carpenter to spite her lover.

Dr. Park Dietz says that obsessed fans of celebrities "actually have an unholy alliance with the tabloids." Many fans and stalkers depend on the tabloids for personal details of celebrities' lives and whereabouts.

According to Dr. Walt Risler, a University of Indiana professor and nationally recognized expert on obsessed star fans, the tabloids and tabloid television play up the fantasies of the already obsessed fan in a way that is potentially dangerous:

> Tabloids are already part of the lives of celebrity stalkers. When they validate their delusions, they are lighting a fire under a combustible situation.

So, what we are *really* talking about from the stars' viewpoint is defense against the *unwanted* star stalkers. Some star stalkers are highly desired, but those with evil intent are not. How to spot them and tell the difference. Certainly one early warning system focuses on the fan mail received by any star or public figure.

Realistically, there is no absolutely foolproof way to protect a celebrity from a stalker, just as there is no foolproof way of keeping an assassin from killing the President if the assassin is willing to die in the process.

However, fan letters are almost always the first contact made by the stalker to the star.

These can be a good insight into the mental state of the fan or stalker and what his or her intentions are. Stalker specialist Gavin de Becker believes that most fans are harmless so long as they limit their contacts with the star to fan mail. It is when the fan tries to make personal contact that possible dangers sharply increase. The mail that fans write is a clue to whether or not he or she will attempt personal contact.

So, for some celebrities, fan mail is now more carefully scrutinized with agents and mail screeners carefully watching for threats— even veiled threats. David Brokaw has made a career out of screening very visible celebrities' mail for over twenty years:

> If we get a threatening letter, the first thing we do is make the client and additional representatives aware of it. If it's something we feel concerns us, we go to the authorities and report it. In my years in the business, we have received only three or four that have concerned me. I've always called the FBI.

Dick Grant is another professional celebrity mail screener who works for Joan Rivers, Larry Hagman, and Richard Dreyfuss:

We get several hundred pieces of fan mail a week. We have people who read through it. If it's regular mail, it goes to a fan mail service for photos. If it's personal, a letter about a terminally ill child who wants to meet a star, it's referred to the star's office. If it's threatening, it goes to the FBI.

Dale Olsen whose clients include Dyan Cannon, Shirley MacLaine, and Sally Kirkland outlines what his readers look for:

You have to look at the way it is written. If it's very intelligently written, grammatically correct and appears to come from someone who has a clear idea, then it can be dangerous. If the letter is from someone who is less educated, I think more often than not it's just a fantasy and you don't react to it.

Some of the other things that de Becker looks for in fan mail is how the writer sees himself and how the writer sees the star. Does he or she see themselves as God or an agent of God; or, do they see themselves as the star's protector, lover, or salvation? Those are all danger signs of mental instability, hallucination, and obsession. Also, how intense or passionate or driven is the letter and how many have been sent by this person. Intensity and volume are additional warning signs of someone who could become a serious threat.

De Becker also tries to deal with the star stalker in a preventive way through a computer program he invented with a colleague. It is called MOSAIC and it contains the profiles of several thousand people who might want to kill or injure one of his clients. With a staff of twenty-one, his organization tries to keep track of these potential threats, their locations, and their activities. They get help from police, media reports, mental hospital staff, and even the families of the star stalkers who want to keep their relative from doing something terrible and being punished for it.

One example of the problem of protecting people from stalkers rests with how the U.S. government helps stalkers find their victims. For years, it was possible to find out a person's new mailing address from their old mailing address by paying the U.S. Postal Service a $3 fee. If a stalking victim was moving residences to get away from a stalker, the U.S. Postal Service would help the stalker keep track of his or her victim.

In 1992 Congress investigated this practice and found postal information such as addresses is sold and resold thousands of times to mailing list brokers, credit bureaus, advertisers, and almost anybody that wants them. Some forty million people move every year and most of them file Change of Address cards. What they don't know is that the information on those Change of Address cards has been publicly available unless you go through the time and expense of getting a court order blocking the information about you.

At the beginning of January 1994, the Postmaster General, Marvin Runyon, announced the problem would be taken care of and there was no need to worry.

However, Postmaster Runyon is the victim of a bureaucratic mind-set that is common throughout the world. Whenever a problem comes up, the professional politician or bureaucrat tends to react by giving the appearance of doing something without actually doing anything.

In Postmaster Runyon's case, he has banned selling address information to the public for $3, but he still is allowing the information to be sold to mailing list companies and credit bureaus. Since anybody can order a credit report that has the address, phone number, and other information on almost anybody in America from a commercial credit bureau for $35 to $100, nothing has been done except to make stalking a little more expensive.

Thirteen

Joni was a star stalker in love with a female star.

Joni Leigh Penn had gotten onto the set of *Cagney & Lacey* many times and seemed to be a normal, well-behaved, adoring fan. However, all that changed. During the next four years, Penn sent Sharon Gless over one hundred obsessive letters ranging from romantic to hostile to ones saying all she wanted in life was to be near the star.

One letter had three very disturbing photos enclosed. One of the pictures was of a shrine to Gless decorated with flowers and photos of the star and an assault rifle right in the middle of it all. Another showed Penn with a pistol pressed against her head and a third had Penn with the pistol in her mouth as if to blow her brains out the back of her head.

An alarming letter was received by Gless in January 1988 from a psychiatrist who had Penn in therapy. Dr. Hubert Nestor wrote that Penn planned "to shoot herself in front of you. This might put you in danger although such is not the motive of this patient and legally I must inform a citizen when this is the case."

The letters from Penn continued, and in September there was an unwelcome visit by Penn to Gless's home which prompted Gless to get a court order in November 1988 ordering Penn to keep one thousand yards away from Gless or her residences. Like most of such stay-away orders, it was useless in real life.

1989-90 had been a difficult period for Gless because her father had been in declining health and in the hospital all the time. During the last year of shooting *Cagney & Lacey,* Gless would visit her father in the hospital every night after work even if it was two or three in the morning.

The bittersweet conclusion came when she was with him as he died and he muttered his final words, "I didn't think you'd be here." She was warm inside from having been there at the last when she was needed, but it was still emotionally draining.

Cagney & Lacey wrapped up after several years of production, and the next day an exhausted Sharon Gless checked herself into a convalescent home for an extended stay to recuperate from the strains of that final year.

It was a lucky decision because it meant that

she wasn't at home at 3:15 A.M. on March 30, 1990, when Penn broke into Gless's San Fernando Valley home through a window. Her intent was to assault Sharon sexually, murder her, and then commit suicide. What she didn't know was that she had tripped a silent alarm and soon there were two Los Angeles police officers in the house.

Sergeant Richard Thomas said: "They went into the home and they were confronted by the woman. She pointed the gun at herself and threatened to kill herself. She then moved back into the bathroom and locked the door."

She was armed with a semiautomatic rifle and more than five hundred rounds of ammunition. Captain Dan Watson reported that the police at the house called for backup in the form of a SWAT team. The SWAT team arrived and police went around the neighborhood evacuating the people nearby. One neighbor, Susan Cascio, said: "We just heard this pounding on the door in the middle of the night and were told there was a crazy lady with a gun. It was scary."

A special police negotiator was brought in, but Joni refused to talk with him because he was a man. Police officer Patricia Stark was substituted and they talked through the rest of the night and into the morning from a telephone in the bathroom, where Joni often turned the subject to suicide. After seven hours, the officer said Joni was getting tired and she gave up about ten A.M. and surrendered the weapons she had purchased a year before. She had only a few cuts on her hand from broken glass.

By the time the sun had come up on this quiet residential street, the neighborhood had become a nightmare of reporters, TV vans with antennae sprouting to the sky, cameras and tripods, and mobs of people milling around. It was like a scene from *Cagney & Lacey* without the two stars.

Later investigation into Joni's background revealed that she lived in the Orange County community of Santa Ana some forty or fifty miles south of Gless's home in a two-bedroom apartment with her twin sister, Jeanni. Neighbors said she earned a living cleaning houses and they were surprised at what had happened because Joni was so quiet and withdrawn.

Joni Leigh pled no contest to felony burglary, apologized to Sharon Gless with whom she said she was in love, and was sentenced to six years in prison in 1990. A judge reduced that to four years and she was released less than two years later. The sentence reduction was part of a plea-bargain deal under which her lawyer, Mitchell J. Bruckner, a deputy public defender, said she might have

served nine years and eight months if convicted after a trial and also because Penn
apologized to Sharon Gless during her sen-
tencing hearing.

San Fernando Superior Court judge John
H. Major cut Penn's sentence on the basis of
a good progress report from the California
Department of Corrections that said she had
been a model prisoner in the California Institute for Women in Frontera. She had not
created problems for the guards or other
prisoners and was thought to have learned
her lesson. When it was all done, Penn was
paroled in 1992.

Joni Leigh Penn works in an halfway house
restaurant, The John Henry Cafe, in Orange
County while remaining under medication
and therapy. The John Henry Cafe is staffed
with a number of parolees such as Joni Leigh
and it adjusts their work schedules to accom-
modate their mood swings and medication
needs. It is a constructive way of allowing disturbed people another chance to get rehabili-
tated in a normal environment.

Fourteen

Sports stalkers are usually both those obsessed with loving the victim and those obsessed with the victim's sports competitor.

International sports stars who have been victims of stalkers include tennis players Monica Seles and Annabel Croft, as well as skater Katarina Witt.

"My life is a prison," said Monica Seles in 1991. "It gets pretty scary sometimes." The painful truth of her perception came clear on April 30 when a loner with a crazed desire to promote the fortunes of Seles's main competitor, Steffi Graf, who ironically has also been the victim of celebrity stalkers during her career. He leapt up at courtside and plunged a nine-inch serrated boning knife into Monica's back.

The assailant, Gunter Parche, had been stalking Seles for weeks waiting for the right moment to attack. An unemployed lathe operator, he had turned his room in the attic of his aunt's house in Gorsbach, Germany, into a Steffi Graf shrine filled with posters and videos of his idol.

Parche, who initially was not identified in full since German law forbids publication of last names of people accused of a crime, did what he felt had to be done so that his adored Steffi Graf would get what is "rightfully" hers.

There had been gossip around the closed world of professional tennis that Seles was the target of politically motivated death threats. Although she has lived in the U.S. since 1986, she was born and raised in the Serbian part of what used to be Yugoslavia. Because she refuses to take a public stand on the vicious civil war going on in her homeland, she has been the target of some zealots who regard her as a traitor.

Seles now just wants to be left alone to live her life and pursue her tennis career. "There are so many rumors out there. I love this game too much. I just want to get back, hit the ball have fun and go forward with my life."

Annabel Croft, the British tennis star who retired in 1988, was stalked during much of her career. "When I was playing there were always cases of weirdos who would turn up at every single venue."

This is true of athletic stars in every kind of sport, including someone who seems not easily intimidated like Chicago Bulls star Michael Jordan. "If you're in the spotlight, you have to think about that."

Richard Barthol is a sports psychologist who is based at UCLA and has studied the phenomenon of stalking and fan obsession with sports celebrities:

> There has been an enormous increase in all kinds of violence. It seems to me this is not related to sports; this is related to celebrity or prominence. For some reason, there are some people who attack celebrities. It's just a manifestation of the way the world is.

Katarina the Great was her nickname in East Germany, and she was the greatest athlete that Communist country had produced in some years.

The beautiful and talented skater has had an impressive amateur career winning six European women's skating championships, five world championships, and two Olympic gold medals between 1982 and 1988. She is now a professional figure skater who headlines international ice shows and regularly competes in sanctioned professional events.

Some of the rewards she garnered as an amateur Olympian included a Lada sports car with its own cellular telephone and an expensive wardrobe. To her confusion, these special perks stirred a lot of resentment among her countrymen; this was before East Germany's reunification with West Germany. People wanted to know why she had been given a four-room apartment in East Berlin and bonuses of $3,725 during a three-month period when families with children had a lot smaller apartments and schoolteachers only earned $90 a month.

None of that resentment, however, terrified her as much as the solitary love of an unemployed crop duster named Harry Veltman III. He was an obsessive stalker hunting down two-time Olympic figure-skating gold medalist, Katarina Witt. She had been swamped with 35,000 love letters after she won the Olympic Gold Medal at the 1984 games in Sarajevo, but Harry Veltman was different.

For nearly two years the divorced schizophrenic had lived with his mother in Westminister, California, and deluged Katarina with one hundred obscene love letters, marriage proposals, nude photos of himself, a Bible, and, when convinced of her rejection, death threats.

It didn't matter to Harry. He knew he was right and doing what God had intended for him to do with his life. He told people about his devotion to Katarina and said, "I was willing to march into hell for a heavenly cause."

In 1990, he sold his pickup truck to get the money for a seven-week trip to Katarina's home in Altenhof, Germany, where he would jump over the fence at three in the morning, pound on the door yelling over and over again, "I love you," and conclude by masturbating on her doorstep.

At the end of December 1991, the FBI finally agreed to arrest him after he sent her a letter containing words they construed as a death threat:

> Please don't be afraid when God allows me to pull you out of your body to hold you tight! Then, you'll know there is life beyond the flesh.

Katarina had to appear in court against Harry and said beforehand that she was just shaking with fear going in, but pulled herself together enough to testify that she feared for her life and was terrified of Harry. That convinced the jury, one of whom voted to convict because Harry showed no signs of remorse at what he had done to frighten Katarina. Harry's distraught mother was convinced it was the pesticides Harry worked with that made him lose touch. "I know Harry would never have hurt her. It's a tragedy for both of them."

But for the forty-seven-year-old possessed with passion for Katarina, his possibly being sentenced to up to thirty years in prison was worth it. He was convicted of four charges of sending obscene material through the mail and two of sending threatening material to Witt. Fortunately, for Harry, the judge didn't come down that hard on him.

On June 3, 1992, he was sentenced by a Santa Ana, California, court to thirty-seven months in a mental hospital. When he is finally released, he will be on three years' probation, but all of this will probably do nothing to stem his obsession with Witt.

A year-and-a-half later, at about 2:30 on the afternoon of January 6, 1994, 24-year old figure skating champion Nancy Kerrigan of Plymouth, Massachusetts, had just completed her practice session at the Cobo ice rink in Detroit for the U.S. Figure skating championships to qualify for the 1994 Winter Olympics in Norway. She went behind a curtain on the way to her dressing room and paused to talk with Pittsburgh Post-Gazette reporter, Dana Scarton, when a stalker struck.

He wielded a heavy metal club and beat Kerrigan around the legs and knee caps in an attempt to serious cripple her. The 6 foot 2 inch attacker weighed about 200 pounds and pounced on the championship skater without warning and said nothing throughout the vicious assault, while the stricken Kerrigan screamed, "Why me? Why me?"

After pounding Kerrigan with the lethal club, the assailant turned and raced through a tunnel under the stands to a rear door that was chained shut and smashed out the Plexiglas to escape into the crowd of people attending the International Auto Show next door.

Just before the attack, a man carrying a video camera came up to one of the coaches, Frank Carroll and asked who Kerrigan was. Carroll indicated who she was and didn't think much about it although he did think the man was acting a little weird.

"The next thing I heard," said Carroll, "was Nancy screaming, screaming, screaming."

Another coach, Kathy Stuart, said that she had noticed this suspicious-looking guy with a hat and coat on and sweating a lot while he sat in the stands by the skating rink videotaping Nancy.

At first everybody thought that the man who attacked Nancy was a stalker following the normal stalker pattern of deep love and attachment followed by anger when he thought she had spurned his affection. She was, in fact, being stalked and got two letters from a ardent fan in Ontario, Canada, after her appearance in the 1992 Olympics. Mary Scotvold, one of Nancy's coaches, saw the letter and said it was overly complimentary and, she thought, bordered on the obscene. Nancy decided not to answer the letter or to send a photograph as she normally would have done.

Then, a year later, came a second letter from the same fan who was angry because she had failed to answer the first letter. She had rejected him and he damn well didn't like it. However, there were no specific threats in this second letter that would directly alarm anyone, Nancy thought, but she turned both letters over to the police as a precaution anyhow. Kerrigan's agent, Jerry Solomon, said they had received a lot of nutty letters, but that was normal for the life of a celebrity and they hadn't received anything that made them particularly nervous.

A few days later, the case changed in a way that nobody expected. Nancy was a victim, not of a stalker, but of a plot motivated by a competitor who wanted to be somebody and who thought Nancy was denying her that.

Tonya Harding also has been the target of a stalker. She was the mark of a stalker who sent her death threats at the 1991 U.S. national figure skating champion and a member of the 1992 Olympic team. She pulled out of the Northwest regional championship competition in her hometown of Portland, Oregon, on November 4, 1993.

Janet Evans, Olympic swimming star, has gotten many letters from a man who seems obsessed with her to the point of sending letters about her to newspapers.

Fifteen

"P.S . . . I'll bet you don't know what would happen if you skinned a person and ate him. If you come bring some big people with you. I've had this urge to eat my best friend for the past nine years."

That's what one Hollywood star was written by a stalker. It is not particularly unique.

We've heard from those who manage the fan mail of celebrities and the kind of guidelines they have. Now we look at the research of a group of psychiatric experts and what they found from analyzing 1,800 letters to Hollywood stars from 214 people. That's an average of eight letters from each potential stalker, although some have literally written hundreds or thousands of letters. The record is held by one woman who has stalked a Hollywood star for years and written over ten thousand letters to the celebrity.

The letters analyzed came from the archives of Gavin de Becker, and the objective was to discern the characteristics and patterns in these letters between the 107 letter writers who, after writing letters, attempted to contact the star or pursue the star, and the 107 other letter writers who *did not* attempt to contact or pursue the star.

The point being to give the security people some concrete clues from the letters as to who might be physically dangerous because of wanting to physically connect with the stars and, perhaps, hurt or kill them.

The analysis team was able to isolate fifteen factors in these 1,800 letters that they believe can predict whether or not the letter writer will try to make a dangerous contact with the star.

The team's first finding was surprising. Whether or not the letter writer made threats in his or her letter had no bearing on whether or not the letter writer would stalk and try to make physical contact with the star. In short, a written threat to a star from a stalker does not necessarily mean there will be an attempt to carry it out.

As in all scientific studies the analysts here are careful to define their words so everybody understands what is being tested and what the results are.

For example, they don't talk simply about a letter sent to the star but, rather, about some form of transmission other than phone calls. That might include letters, postcards, telegrams, faxes, diaries, scripts, flowers, gifts, and so on.

As for coming near the star or trying to make physical contact in a way that might be dangerous to the star, they list six different actions by the stalker that would qualify as being called "pursuing" the star:

- going to the star's home
- going to the star's agent
- visiting home or business of someone close to the star
- coming within five miles of any of the above with intent of physical contact
- traveling more than three hundred miles to see the star in person or in a public appearance
- acting unusual at a star's public appearance

Here is a sampling of the kinds of letters and communications the analytical team studied:

Middle-aged male fan to young singer:

I am afraid I made a mistake when I told you I was your father. Some guy showed me a picture of you and your father standing together when you got your award.

I was so proud when I thught (sic) I

was your pop. I guess that means that my daughter aint (sic) your sister either.

I asked your manager to borrow $10,000 I hope she lets me have it. Before I go I just want to say the the only reason I thought I was your pop was because I used to got (sic) with a person that looked like you.

Love forever

A male fan to a woman star:

Hello darling this is youre (sic) New friend . . . we will be soon together for our love honey, I will write and mail lovely photo of myslef okay. I will write to you Soon, have a lovely Easter time hoping to correspond . . . here is a postcard for you . . . honey how are you doing . . . wishing to correspond with you Soon . . . hoping we do some camping and Barbecueing Soon okay

From a mental patient and murderer to an actress whom the writer believed was being held captive and starved by the police:

Please disregard the other letter [I sent in January] I sent to you. Disregard this letter if you are married or have a boyfriend, as I don't want to break up an existing relationship. I would like you to be one of the following to me; (a) a lover, (b) a girlfriend, or (c) a wife. I want it to be a forever thing, if we have faith in each other, and don't cheat. You must fulfill the following; (1) you must be a vegetarian (2) you must not have another boyfriend. (3) You must not hold hands or do anything beyond that point, with another, unless I give you permission (4) I believe in birth control devices and [fetus removal] abortion, to take the fear away from women, so they can have a complete orgasm. Men never have to worry, because they, don't have the baby. (5) You must not wear pants, unless the temperature drops below 50 degrees F. or you engage in hazardous work [like coal mining]. (6) You can view pornographic movies.

. . . I was in a gunfight with the police, because I thought you didn't have to eat food. I was real sick [crazy] at the time. I was arrested, but should be getting out soon. I'm in a hospital; for observation. I was wounded as was one policeman. We are both okay now. A bystander was wounded by another policeman.

. . . I'm a vegetarian. I believe the slaughter of innocent animals is a crime against humanity . . .

. . . last chance. Let's sit in a little

room together. Let's drive to the end of the world. Let's look in each others eyes. Let's magnetically attract each other from close up. Let's talk till we want each other more than anyone else . . . I believe we can have a good life together. Please call, write or come here by February 6th or else I'll have to look for someone else . . ."

One of America's well-known female TV stars got this letter from one of her fans:

. . . I would like to Have lots of pictures of you sex symBol woman like you are all the times if you don't mine at all if you take off your clotHes for me and I can see wHat you Got to the world then ever that love any How I would like to know How LonG is your Breast any-How I would like to know How mucH milk Do you carry in your Breast any-How I would like to know How far Does your Breast stic out on you anyHow I By playBoy Books all the times . . . I would like you to put up your legs and take pictures of you in the nude . . . I would like Have larGe pictures of you in tHe nude lots of them then ever were so I will take with me and have lots of womens in tHe nude I like sex symBol womens to look at all times.

* * *

In checking these letters and other communications against the incidence of approaching or pursuing of the star, the team found a direct correlation between the frequency that a stalker wrote with the probability that he or she would try physical contact with the star. In the sample studied, those writers who did not try to physically connect with the star wrote an average of a little more than four letters. Those who did try to make physical contact wrote an average of almost ten letters— more than twice as many as the nonpursuers. So frequence of writing is one of the signs of a stalker who will try to make physical contact with the star. It is not the only sign, though.

The length of the letters didn't seem to make enough of a difference that it could be used as a significant sign. However, the length of time the writer had been writing did. Those who had been writing and sending things to the star for more than a year were more likely to make contact than those who had done it for less than a year.

The content of the communications was, as one might suspect, significant. Oddly, eighty-four percent of those writing gave their full names, and eighty-six percent addressed the star by name. The experts' conclusion was that anonymous letters were from people who were no more dangerous than letters where the writer was fully identified.

While most of the letters came from one fixed return address including those in Europe and the Philippines, the fact that forty-four percent of the return addresses were in just three states: New York, California, and Texas.

There seemed to be nothing particularly significant about the type of paper or ink or style of handwriting or typing. Most letters were handwritten or typed. That exploded a common myth about stalker's letters, almost none of them [one percent] were made up of letters cut out of magazines and newspapers and pasted on a page.

The most unusual part of these communications is that most of them had something enclosed which spanned from the mild to the strange [fifty-five percent]. Just to get an idea of the sorts of things included in these letters: Twenty-three percent had drawings, poetry, and tapes, and eighteen percent had photos of the writer, none of which seems particularly odd for a fan letter.

However, if you want odd, consider some of the other things that were tucked in the fans' letters received by stars. A short, random list includes:

- dog teeth
- bedpan
- syringe of blood

- animal excrement
- toy submarine
- facsimile bomb
- copy of *Texas Monthly* magazine
- driver's license
- a coyote's head
- half-eaten candy bar
- disposable razor
- pack of cigarettes
- six comic books
- four $100 bills in play money
- medical photos of corpses with star's face pasted on
- blood-smeared paper
- three playing cards

As weird as some of this junk seems to be, the investigators couldn't find a connection between any of these things and the possibility of approaching the star and being a threat.

Most writers wanted something from the star and it was usually acknowledgment of the writer's existence or importance to the star. A total of seventy-nine percent wanted to meet with the star or get a letter or phone call. About half of these wanted a face-to-face meeting with the star, and this group was considered a significant threat to the star.

As one might expect, many of the writers

dwelt on romantic and sexual subjects and most were aroused by the star. The letter writers talked about all sorts of romantic involvements such as being a lover, spouse, or having children with the star. Of sex, every imaginable form is mentioned in some of the letters, but the most commonly mentioned is vaginal intercourse and fellatio. Interestingly, the research team concluded that writers who dwell on marrying, having sex or children with the star are *less likely* to try making a dangerous personal contact.

Particular attention, of course, was paid to those writers making threats to the star. These threats, however, were sometimes direct ["I will kill you"] and sometimes implied ["Something may happen to you"] and often obscured in some unclear symbolism or curse such as:

I don't know what else to tell you. I've warned you. Repent and accept Christ before the hour of God's Wrath upon the world arrives. It will be a Holocaust like the world has never seen.

You better not get your hair cut because if you do— Jupiter will collide with Mars.

May the veins in your legs get darker,

bluer, and uglier; and bigger; and hideous;— like your repulsive body.

Write that letter to me God Damn It or else I'll have you all fornicating with Ubangies before I'm through with you— and I mean it!

I realize that you aren't going to come looking for me. So, I'm going to have to go looking for you. Please don't be frightened. I am not a nut.

I saw your movie you looked at me at the last of the picture, now I am going to do something else with my time. This was not in this letter last time! You will see.

Of the threatening letters, the most common focus was the star and the second most common was the threatening letter writer. Most of the writers said they would carry out their threats themselves. What they were going to do, in the order of frequency, was kill the star, maim or mutilate the star sexually, hurt the star in some other way, and destroy their career.

In summing up the study done by the research group— analyzing the content, theme, physical components, frequency, and special characteristics— the team came up with sixteen factors that it believes are warning signs of a potentially dangerous stalker of Hollywood stars.

The major factors that make the writer more likely a danger include these:

- the number of communications received
- correspondence or contact for more than a year
- saying the writer wants to meet the star personally
- setting a time for something to happen to the star
- telephoning the star in addition to writing
- letters with different postmarks

The different postmarks indicate that the writer is on the move and not easy to locate. [He usually doesn't give his or her full name and return address as most of the letter writers do.] Pushing for a meeting, setting deadlines, and telephoning suggest increased intensity of the emotional tension in the writer which may be pushing him or her to take action. The continued correspondence for over a year indicates a long-term commitment to this obsession and one in which the writer has a great deal of time, effort, and emotion invested. Therefore, it is not one he or she is willing to abandon easily.

The most surprising conclusion of the team was there is little connection between threats and dangerous physical behavior. As the team reported:

> This finding [lack of connection between threatening words and dangerous behavior] contradicts a vast body of assumptions that is relied on each day in judging whether harassing communications warrant concern, notification of the police, security precautions or investigation . . . Those who rely on the presence or absence of threats in making judgments about what to do are making a serious mistake.

Unfortunately, not only are celebrity letter screeners making that mistake, but so is the law because that mistaken assumption is written into most antistalking laws.

Sixteen

Lynette "Squeaky" Fromme was a woman with very low self-esteem, who needed the attention and approval of someone she worshiped. In Fromme's case her obsession was with the evil guru Charles Manson, who had inspired the stalking and bloody murder of Sharon Tate.

As with many stalkers, Fromme left behind a diary that helps track her stalking. She grew up in Santa Monica, California, took ballet lessons, was a cheerleader, and listened to the Beach Boys endlessly. She graduated from high school in 1967 and was in conflict with her straight-arrow aeronautical engineer father.

One day she and her father had a terrible quarrel and he ordered her out of the house and told her never to come back. Frightened and abandoned, she went down to the Venice beach near her home and sat down on a bench overlooking the surf and desperately wondered what to do. She had the two things that mattered most at the moment when she fled her father's house, her schoolbooks and her eye makeup.

What she later described as "an elfish, dirty-looking creature" with a luminous smile came over to her and said, "So, your father kicked you out." Startled by his insight, she let him sit and talk with her, and he got her to relax, laugh, and feel there was still hope for her. Then, he got up and began walking away, inviting her to come with him and be part of what he was:

> He smiled a soft feeling and was on his way. I grabbed my books, running to catch up with him. I didn't know why— I didn't care— and I never left.

In the months that followed, Lynette felt that she had met both a new father and the incarnation of Jesus Christ. Later much was made about the free and easy sex in the Manson Cult or Manson Family, but that was secondary in importance to many of the women in the group like Fromme.

Fromme described her feeling, "I felt so close to him and laid my head on his shoulder, wanting a daddy to hold me . . . As all daughters I had wanted all the attention I could get from my daddy."

Her need for a daddy was focused on Manson, but she also would connect with other older men when it was necessary. She maintained a close relationship with eighty-one-year-old George Spahn, the owner of the ranch out in the west end of the San Fernando Valley where the Manson Family made their home.

She was also involved with a sixty-five-year-old retiree, who gave her money and let her use his car. He also gave her a .45-caliber pistol that she kept with her belongings and would later use to help the obsessive center of her life, Charles Manson.

She was not involved in the stalking and murders of the Tate-La Bianca case; certainly, those involved were largely there because of their devotion to Manson and need to get his approval and approbation.

Most of the members of his "Family" were white women in their late teens and early twenties who were obsessed by him and believed he was either Jesus Christ or God and that his twisted philosophical blend of Beatles lyrics, the Book of Revelations, satanism, Scientology, and Nazi beliefs were the revealed word of God.

Manson's objective was to achieve total power over society. His strategy, naive and stupid at best, was to stalk and slaughter important and powerful white people as an example to the oppressed but childlike black race. This, Manson preached, would inspire these blacks to rise up and kill all the whites in America and create what he dubbed "Helter Skelter." He borrowed that term from a track on the Beatles' "White Album." However, once having done that, these simpleminded, guileless black people would be bewildered at how to rule themselves. Then, Charles Manson would be summoned from the desert to become "King of America."

Manson and four of his disciples went to prison for the Tate-La Bianca murders, but it left most of the Family, still obsessed with their devotion to Manson, floating at odds—including Lynette Fromme.

In some ways, Fromme may have felt guilty that she hadn't killed for her father figure, lover, holy savior, and guru like the others had done. The others were special beings blessed by sharing the fate of their Christ and Daddy. Lynette was driven by the need to do something that would make her important in Manson's eyes.

She decided that she needed to do something to please him, and nothing would please him more than if she could get the world to listen to his preaching.

While she tried to work out how to do that, she and two other Manson women, Sandra Good and Susan Murphy, moved to Sacramento near the state capitol building. Living off a small trust fund Good had and money from friends, they began stalking and helping others stalk the heads of various polluting corporations such as the president of the Kaiser Company, William Roesch.

Fromme wrote letters to another of their group, Edward Vandervort, in Pennsylvania, spelling out what to do in stalking and killing Roesch:

Muster up your meanest voice, think of your dying world and call. Speak slowly and precisely and clearly and as mean and frightening as you can. I know you'll do it good. Tell them the following: "Your product is killing, poisoning the world. There is no excuse for it."

[Now say this slowly]: "If you do not stop killing us, Manson will send for your heart . . . Or watch your own blood spell out your crime on the wall. Remember Sharon Tate."

This letter of instructions was followed by one even more ominous also guiding Vandervort in dealing with Roesch:

Ed,
I just sent you a list of corporations to call. This one is to take care of NOW. William Roesch— President of Kaiser

Company, makers of more forms of pollution than I can count— sellers of lives and souls— killers of U.S. more than anyone.

William Roesch

With an address in Bridgeville, Pennsylvania. Do not threaten him first. Kill him. Destroy him. Here's How.

Case it out. Check for kids. We want to avoid hurting any kids. But get him and the wife however you can. Use gloves.

Be careful and sly. Could wear paint clothes. Take with you an aerosol can of BAN deodorant. Take also a can of pink paint and a large paint brush.

When bodies are dead, paint as much as you can of them with PINK paint. [faces, arms, etc.]

Put the aerosol can in the man's mouth.

Do not write anything about Helter Skelter or any other words you got out of that book. Or, anything about Manson.

Vandervort chickened out— -and Fromme realized that only she was committed enough to do what needed to be done to give Charles Manson honor and to get his message to the world.

* * *

In June 1975 she wrote to L.A. Judge Raymond Choate and asked him to reduce Manson's sentence so that he could get out and preach salvation to the world before it was too late. That, thought Fromme, would please Manson. When the judge didn't do anything, Fromme called and threatened his children and warned that she was going to do something desperate to free her lover, her father, her Christ.

To impress and serve Charlie Manson she was willing to do anything, stalk anybody, pursue any course. She and Good began wearing red robes to get attention to their message that their beloved Manson must be freed to save the earth:

> We're nuns now, and we wear red robes. We're waiting for our Lord [Manson] and there's only one [thing] to do before he comes off the cross [prisons] and that's clean up the earth. Our red robes are an example of new morality. We must clean up the air, the water and the land. They're red with sacrifice, the blood of sacrifice.

In August 1975 Fromme began a correspondence with Chuck Rossi, a reporter at NBC. She hoped that Rossi would give media coverage to Manson's philosophy because she was sure that would immediately trigger a public outcry for a new trial and vindication of her Lord:

The media CAN be used to unwind the tangles of a world running in circles toward what it fears most. Manson can explain the self-destructive thought. He can explain the Christ thought. But he must have the opportunity to bring this message of salvation to the world otherwise our lives will terminate in the drug store, booze bottles and morgues of a decadent and polluted Tate-La Bianca society.

If Manson is not allowed to explain, there will be many more young murderers beginning with the person typing this letter.

The Manson Family had stalked the Tate houseguests and the La Bianca family and slaughtered them. Fromme had played a part in stalking industrialists in the name of getting freedom and an audience for the Lord with whom she was obsessed. Now came another chance to prove her love and her devotion and to give Manson an audience, she would stalk the President of the United States. That would please Charlie.

Fromme learned that President Ford was

going to visit Sacramento and she checked
out his arrival at the Senator Hotel across the
street from the state capitol. After that, she
went home, and got her red robe and the
.45 Harold Boro had given her.

The next morning, September 5, 1975, she
staked out the Senator Hotel and watched
Ford and his entourage emerge at 9:45. The
group began walking across the street and
the forest-like capitol grounds toward the
gilt-domed structure. As the group moved,
spectators and fans eddied around the edges
waving and speaking greetings to the President.

The genial Ford returned the waves and
the greetings and quickly noticed a petite,
young woman in a red gown and red turban
moving along with them at the edge of his
escort group. She shifted closer and closer
and moved slightly ahead of where the President was walking in the center of his escort.

Then, the childlike young woman turned
and stepped boldly into the path of the President until she was just two feet from him
and they were literally face-to-face. She
fished into her robe and produced the pistol
that she aimed right at Jerry Ford's genitals.

Stunned, Ford stopped, bewildered by what
to do because he couldn't flee since his reti-
nue of aides and Secret Service bodyguards
hemmed him in and, literally, held him en-
trapped confronting his assassin.

The nature of her pistol was that the hammer was pulled back in cocked position so as to fire with the least delay. Seeing the danger and seeing the pistol cocked back and everybody being close and practically on top of each other, a Secret Service man instantly wrapped his hand around the back of the pistol in such a way that the web between his thumb and forefinger would keep the hammer from driving home and exploding the cartridge in the chamber. His colleagues grabbed Fromme and threw her to the ground quickly.

She was tried in the U.S. District Court of Judge Thomas J. McBridge, but refused to participate in any way. She tried to plead guilty and the judge refused the plea and ordered a trial in which she did nothing more than watch the proceedings on closed-circuit TV. Every morning Judge McBridge would ask her if she wished to participate in the trial and every morning she would say "No" and the judge would say "Thank you" and proceed.

She was found guilty and sentenced to life in prison. She had stalked President Ford to prove her worth to her Lord, Manson, and she succeeded in that. She had hoped to please him further by giving him and his visions a great forum, but she failed in that quest.

* * *

Less than three weeks later, September 22, Sara Jane Moore, a weak, confused, middle-aged divorcée would follow in Fromme's footsteps. Moore had alternately been associated with violent, left-wing radicals and, other times, acted as an FBI informant. Rejected by the FBI and feeling like a piece of monkey dung for betraying her friends, Moore tried to gain reacceptance from her alienated revolutionary friends by trying to shoot President Ford as he left the St. Francis Hotel in San Francisco after giving a speech to the World Affairs Council.

Ironically, her attempt was thwarted by an ex-Marine standing nearby, who grabbed her as she was about to shoot and deflected the shot away from the President. In the media blitz that focused on this hero, it was uncovered and publicized that he was gay. This disclosure ruined his life. He eventually committed suicide in a tacky hotel room several years later. Sara Jane was sentenced to prison for life. She was apparently happy there because she had status inside as a bona fide revolutionary who had stalked and tried to kill the President.

Seventeen

John Hinckley felt it was important to visit Ford's Theater, the site of a legendary national tragedy, a few days before he attempted to assassinate President Ronald Reagan. This was a stalker whose obsession what not with the person he tried to kill. It was with someone else.

John W. Hinckley, Jr., was in love with an unobtainable woman of whom he was not worthy. He was obsessed with Jodie Foster and wanted to make himself famous so that she could love him as he loved her.

He decided one way to become famous was to kill someone famous. So, John Hinckley, a young man with low self-esteem, became a stalker of Presidents. If you kill a President, you go down in history. Your biography goes in the encyclopedia. Hinckley set out to stalk and kill himself a President, and the President he had in mind was not Ronald Reagan as many people thought. It was initially Jimmy Carter.

* * *

John Hinckley, Jr., came into this world in 1955 in the town of Ardmore, Oklahoma, the son of a well-to-do family that soon moved to Dallas where John grew up. In 1973 his father moved his business, Vanderbilt Energy, to Colorado and John enrolled at Texas Tech in Lubbock. He had taken up the guitar and was developing a finely tuned hatred of non-whites along the way.

In 1976, he decided Hollywood was the place for him to break into the music business and become a recording star. He lived in a scruffy apartment in a sleazy section of Hollywood. In spite of optimistic letters to his parents at the beginning, two months into his Hollywood time, he had to ask for financial help.

His parents sent money immediately and he resumed writing optimistic letters about his contacts with United Artists where he was encouraged to form a musical group; his attractive new ladylove, Lynn Collins; and his numerous music business connections. In truth, none of these things existed except in his letters.

He was actually working as a busboy and going to see *Taxi Driver* over and over again at a Hollywood movie palace. He was growing obsessed with the actress Jodie Foster.

After a few more months, he gave up on Hollywood and returned to Texas and started identifying with the National Socialist Party in Dallas: "By the summer of 1978, at the age of twenty-three, I was an all-out anti-Semite and white racist." The following year, he bought a .38-caliber pistol from the Galaxy Pawnshop in Lubbock, went back to Texas Tech, and got involved in several businesses.

One was a newsletter called "American Front," designed for mainstream conservative Americans. Another was a mailing list service, except that he had no inventory to sell. Meanwhile, he bought another gun— a rifle from the Snidely Whiplash Pawnshop— and saw a story in *People* magazine about his idealized woman, Jodie Foster, going to Yale. He had seen *Taxi Driver* fourteen times during his sojourn in Hollywood and memorized her every word and movement in that film.

For quite some time during the period after returning from Hollywood, Hinckley seemed plagued by a series of illnesses including earaches, respiratory problems, and troubles with unspecified anxieties. During this time, he wrote his family:

> My nervous system is about shot. I take heavy medication for it which doesn't seem to do much good except to make me very drowsy. By the end of the summer, I should be a bona fide basket case.

By July 10, his doctor had him on Valium and six days later he stopped by the Galaxy Pawnshop and bought another rifle. This time a .22 caliber. He was also eating a lot and had ballooned up to 222 pounds, and was taking strange photographs of himself including some showing him with one of his guns aimed at his own head.

In August his parents asked him to come home— not because they missed him or wanted to have him hanging around or thought he needed some help in getting his life on track, but because they needed a house-sitter while they traveled to Europe.

Hinckley obliged and had some long conversations in Colorado with a psychologist who did work for his father's company about what to do with his life. Perhaps this was a subtle parental setup to get him counseling help without making an issue of it and generating resentment from their son.

The psychologist, Darrell Benjamin, concluded that Hinckley was emotionally retarded and was a fourteen-year-old trapped in the body of a twenty-five-year-old. He recommended that Hinckley sit down and make a plan of what to do with his life before it was done for him by circumstances.

When his parents returned from their European trip, they and John entered into a formal written agreement about John's immediate future. They would let him sell some of the stock he had been given in trust in his family's company, Vanderbilt Energy, and he would use the money to resume his college education. It sounded like a good idea, but John was working on his own agenda.

The stock sale generated $3,600 and the school John picked to attend was, coincidentally, Yale where his dream woman was attending classes. In September he arrived in New Haven, Connecticut. He was about to connect in person with the dream of his young life.

Operating from a room in the main hotel in New Haven, the Sheraton-Park Plaza, on September 17, he set about trying to locate Jodie Foster through the student register at Yale. This was quite easy as open arrangements exist on most college campuses.

On September 20, John Hinckley had the most exciting and devastating experience of his uneventful life. He was actually able to get Jodie Foster's campus telephone number and speak to her on the phone. He was really talking with *her* and was taping the conversation because he wanted to replay it again and again to experience this virginal moment in what he assumed would be their lifelong love relationship.

Sadly, the lady had other plans. She didn't know who this person was calling her, and she certainly had no intention of meeting him for a date. He was not the only one who found it easy to get her number and who had telephoned her. She tried to be firmly polite and to slough off the callers.

The impact on Hinckley was intense. He was ecstatic at the ease with which he got to her and the fact that she would talk to him at all. At the same time, he was stunned that she didn't understand the depth and fervor of his love for her. Two days later, John called Jodie again and the entire experience was repeated, taping and all. As in the pattern of many stalkings, his romantic overtures had been rejected by his love princess, and the pain of the rebuff hurt in ways it was hard to explain.

The curious stalking odyssey of John Hinckley began, which would have him traveling around the country in search of himself or, more importantly, some way of impressing Jodie Foster. His parents were uneasy about what was happening and continued to try helping him, but he was legally an adult and they couldn't force help on him.

After that first experience at Yale, Hinckley's travels took him back to Lubbock, where he bought two more pistols at Snidely Whiplash's; then, to Washington; and after that to Columbus, Ohio. He was stalking President

Jimmy Carter with the intent of become famous by assassination. Once he was famous, Jodie Foster would realize what she had missed when she turned him away.

From Columbus, he rode the bus to Dayton and hung around for a couple of days until Carter appeared at a convention center meeting. He could have shot him there, but changed his mind and simply was among the hundreds who pressed forward and shook the President's hand. Carter never knew that one of those hundreds of hands he shook that day had intended to murder him.

The ache in his heart drew him back to New Haven. Having found out where Jodie Foster lived, he left notes for her under her door. These frightened her and she notified school authorities and the campus security people, but apparently nothing was done.

By that time, John was in Lincoln, Nebraska, to try connecting with an American Nazi he wanted to meet, but that didn't happen and he flew to where he knew Carter would be next, Nashville, Tennessee. Once more Hinckley awoke one morning with the intention of murdering Jimmy Carter, and once more his resolve melted as the sun rose higher in the sky. It was October 9 and he went, instead, to the airport to get a plane to New York. His plans were derailed by an encounter with the police.

The airport security check revealed guns in John's luggage and he was arrested and held by the police for several hours. The police confiscated Hinckley's two .22-caliber pistols and one .38-caliber pistol, fined him $62.50, and let him go so he could fly to New Haven again.

Two days later, he flew to Dallas and stayed at his sister's house, as well as visiting Rockey's Police Equipment store and replenishing his supply of guns. This time, he bought two more .22-caliber pistols and ammunition. Then, three days later, he was back on his way to New Haven. Two days there and on to Washington, D.C., where, close to running out of money, he flew to Denver and his parents' house.

Once back home, he celebrated by taking an overdose of an antidepressant drug, Surmontil, for which he had a prescription. His mother came home and found him zonked out and brought him around. His father was in Africa doing work for a Christian charity group, World Vision. The next step was to get John to psychiatrist Dr. John Hopper to whom Hinckley confessed that he had two overwhelming obsessions: "I have two obsessions in life now: writing and the person we discussed November 4 [Jodie Foster]. I care about nothing else!"

After Thanksgiving, Hinckley sent a warning to the FBI that Jodie Foster was in danger: "There is a plot underway to abduct actress Jodie Foster from Yale University dorm in December or January. No ransom. She's being taken for romantic reasons. This is no joke! I don't wish to get further involved. Act as you wish."

Apparently, the extent of precautions taken as a result of this threat was that the FBI alerted university authorities who, in turn, alerted Ms. Foster.

Next, Hinckley left Denver and flew back to Washington where he visited Ford's Theater and the Blair House where the President-elect, Ronald Reagan, was staying. A few days later, on December 8, 1980, Mark David Chapman gunned down John Lennon as the rock star emerged from a limo to enter his residence, the Dakota, on Central Park West in New York City.

Hinckley boarded the Amtrak train to Penn Station in New York as soon as he could and joined the memorial service for the slain John Lennon in Central Park. A few days later, on December 14, he took the Metro North train out of Grand Central to New Haven and, once more, slipped love notes under

Jodie Foster's door at Yale. Two days after that, he flew back to Colorado where he was starting to get counseling therapy regularly from Dr. Hopper. He stayed there until the middle of January when he telephoned Foster's number at Yale, but didn't get to speak to her.

In addition to continued visits with Dr. Hopper while in Colorado— specifically in the Denver suburban community of Evergreen— he spent a lot of time practicing shooting his various weapons including a new .38-caliber pistol he had acquired. In February, using the name John Hudson, he flew back to New Haven for the eighth time, sneaking in and out of Foster's dorm building and leaving valentines and poems. From there, he went down to Manhattan and had sex with four prostitutes.

On February 14, he decided he would commit suicide since it was Valentine's Day and the valentine he wanted was ignoring him. The altar upon which this martyr's sacrifice should be made in his mind was the entrance to the Dakota, where John Lennon had been murdered nine weeks before. When Lennon died, so did a dream for millions of his fans. What better place for John Hinckley's dream to die.

Hinckley's lack of nerve defeated his intentions once again. When he was finally standing on the sidewalk in front of the Dakota, he chickened out of his suicide. The next day he was in Washington and the day after that in Evergreen and the day after that in New Haven and a few days later, on February 27, back in Evergreen to see Dr. Hopper for the last time.

Two days later, he snuck into where his parents kept their valuables and stole $500 worth of gold Krugerrands, which he converted to dollars at a currency exchange and flew back to New Haven for the tenth time to leave more notes under Jodie's door:

Just wait. I'll rescue you very soon. Please cooperate.

Goodbye! I love you six trillion times. Don't you maybe like me just a little bit. [You must admit I am different.] It would make all of this worthwhile.

At this point, John was out of money and broke in New Haven. As he had done repeatedly, his father got him a plane ticket home, met him at the Denver Airport, gave him some money, and told him to get lost.

He spent the next several days living in motels and selling off his guitar, typewriter and three of his guns to get cash. Then, his mother agreed to drive him to Denver's Stapleton Airport and John flew to Hollywood for a day before hopping a bus to Washington, D.C., where he arrived three days later.

It was March 30 and he woke up to start his day with breakfast at McDonald's and a Valium. Close to noontime he accidentally came across President Reagan's schedule for the day printed in the *Washington Star.*

John took a shower thinking about Jodie and what he needed to do to win her admiration and love. He became agitated to the point that it took another Valium to relax him. He then sat down and wrote a letter to Jodie which he left in his room, number 312, at the Park Central Hotel. Next, he put his .22 loaded with explosive Devastator bullets in his right jacket pocket along with a red John Lennon button in his left pocket and went outside to hail a cab.

The cab dropped him off by the Washington Hilton on Connecticut Avenue just below Columbia Road and he saw where the news reporters were hanging around waiting from the President to finish his speech and come out, so John mingled with them.

At 2:25 P.M., the President and his entourage emerged from the hotel door striding briskly toward the waiting limos, smiling and waving to the bystanders. John Hinckley stepped forward pulling his gun from the jacket pocket, pointed and emptied it in the direction of Ronald Reagan.

The impact of the attempt to kill Reagan was even more dramatic because it was on videotape that revealed a weakness in the Secret Service protection. Videotapes of the President's guards show that all who can be seen were around the President looking at him. They had their backs to where any attack would come from and were, therefore, surprised at the initial assault.

After the shooting began, they all either ducked or finally turned and faced the assailant and smothered him.

In the aftermath, there were only a few notable items of interest. In Hinckley's hotel room were several photos of Jodie Foster, the letter to Jodie Foster, and a hijack note apparently for use on an airplane. This last item was folded up and stuffed into the bottom of a Band-Aid box and it read:

> This plane has been hijacked! I have a bomb with me. Plus flammable liquids and a knife. A companion is also on the plane with a firearm. Act naturally and lead the way to the cabin. Stay calm!

There were also thirty-eight pages of his poems and other writings; pills of Drixoral,

Surmontil, and Valium; and a picture postcard with Ron and Nancy Reagan on one
side and this note to Jodie on the other side:

> Don't they make a darling couple?
> Nancy is downright sexy. One day you
> and I will occupy the White House and
> the peasants will drool with envy. Until
> then, please do your best to remain a
> virgin. You are a virgin, aren't you?

Eighteen

You're going to get a letter from me. You better listen to every word of it and do what it tells you to do or you're gonna be in serious deep trouble and you're not gonna see your daughter again, you hear me? I'm a sick and desperate man and you'll be hearing from me.

It may sound like the dialog out of a bad movie, but it was the voice and threat of the highest judge in the State of New York, Chief Justice Sol Wachtler, threatening the woman he had been stalking for months, Joy Silverman.

Once nominated unsuccessfully by President Bush as the ambassador to Barbados, Silverman, forty-seven, is a rich woman who the media in Manhattan refers to as a "socialite" and who is very active in the high reaches of the Republican party. Wachtler, sixty-four, looks like a judge. He has a full head of hair with a determined face and a deep, I'm-saying-important-things voice that has intoned many decisions from the judicial bench where he sat as the chief justice of the New York State Court of Appeals. Respected, feared and sought after, Wachtler was a man who had come a long way and was marked to go a lot further. However, most people expected him to go to the Governor's mansion in 1994 or some high national office, not the Federal pen in North Carolina.

It began with his arrest on November 7, 1992 by FBI agents who had been assigned to the case for seven weeks. He was charged with blackmail and attempted extortion which were all part of his stalking, though stalking itself is not a federal crime.

Wachtler swamped Silverman with intimidating, unsigned letters and threatening phone calls. None of this was illegal until he started saying he was going to kidnap Silverman's fourteen-year-old daughter and demanding $20,000.

Silverman was married to a New York industrialist, Jeffrey Silver, and during the 1980s they started giving large donations to the national Republican party. President Bush subsequently appointed Joy a trustee of the Kennedy Center for the Performing Arts.

In April of 1992, Joy's astrologer grimly predicted that trouble was coming for Joy's fourteen-year-old daughter, Jessica. The trouble had already begun with threatening and obscene letters.

Years before Joy Silverman had known Sol Wachtler as a family friend, and eight years earlier he had been named the executor of her stepfather's will and $24.8 million estate. This connection earned Sol $500,000 and a long-term, passionate love affair with Joy that lasted until 1991.

This was not the first time Sol had strayed, and Joy was on her third marriage at the time. The daughter of a secretary from Newark, New Jersey, Joy's first husband was Richard Simons, a building contractor by whom she had a son. Then, came David Paul, a Miami bank chairman. Finally, she had settled in with an industrial tycoon, Jeffrey Silverman, whose home-improvement company was one of the *Fortune* Magazine 500 companies.

However, Silverman dumped Sol. Sol was not the sort of man who took rejection well. He retained his calm, professional veneer with his colleagues in the courtroom, but showed another side to Joy.

The venomous, lecherous notes began arriving in April of 1992, some addressed to Joy and some addressed to Jessica. The card to Jessica that arrived in May contained a condom to garnish an obscene message on the card. The next month Joy got a note telling her the writer had compromising and explicit photos of her having sex. The writer also warned that he had hired a private detective, "David Purdy," to get more tapes and more film of the two of them having sex.

This fictitious Purdy now entered the picture. In August, he stopped by the New York apartment of David Samson, a friend of Joy Silverman, and introduced himself to the doorman leaving a message to say "hello" to Samson. He also called Mrs. Samson several times offering to sell her pictures of Joy and David together in bed.

Purdy showed up wearing a cowboy outfit at the Silverman apartment and left a note telling her to put a classified ad in the *New York Times* with a phone number he could call to work out the blackmail deal with her. That was September 12 of 1992.

Since she and her now estranged husband were prominent political contributors, Mrs. Silverman went directly to the Director of the FBI. Director William Sessions assigned eighty agents to solve Joy's problem.

The Silverman apartment was transformed into a branch of the FBI's New York office with special agents camped inside around the clock, telephonic and electronic equipment spilling out all over the place and an air of a besieged bunker.

The first reading the agents had on the source of the anonymous letters with New Jersey postmarks and the threatening phone calls that said the caller was going to do all sorts of terrible things to Joy's fourteen-year-old daughter, Jessica, was wrong. They concluded the source was probably the wife of lawyer, David Samson.

Much to the disappointment of the Bureau, it quickly turned out that Mrs. Samson was not the perpetrator.

Whomever was stalking and threatening Joy was also calling and writing Mrs. Samson. He was taunting Mrs. Samson with stories of the pictures he had of Mr. Samson and Mrs. Silverman in various sexual positions.

The FBI put a tap on Mrs. Silverman's phone and waited. On October 1, 1992 the required ad was placed in the *New York Times* addressed to "Lost Texas Bulldog" with a special phone number for the stalker to call. The stalker did—for an instant and then hung up without saying anything. The electronic equipment the FBI had installed in the Silverman apartment was so sophisticated that even though the connection was broken a few seconds after it rang the line, they were able to instantly get a fix. As soon as one of the agents told Joy the number from which the call came, a chill of painful recognition swept over her. It was the mobile phone number of her ex-lover, Judge Sol Wachtler!

Wachtler was probably unaware mobile phones are simply short-range radio transmitters and receivers. They send and receive messages in the open to and from a wired telephone or transmitter. Anybody with the right kind of scanner or trans-ceiver can listen in and track your calls.

Joy both believed it was Sol and didn't believe he would be so reckless. The FBI reaction was similar. It couldn't be Judge Sol Wachtler.

The FBI needed more proof that it was the judge calling in those threats and sending obscene notes to Joy and Jessica. The orders came directly from William Sessions: treat this like a serious blackmail case.

A few days after that first traced call, came several more calls from a stationary phone location. This time, the judge used a device to distort his voice. He demanded $20,000 for the photos he claimed to have of Joy and David together.

The detectives traced these calls, too, and they all came from public phone booths in the Long Island neighborhood where the Wachtlers lived. The caller had shifted from money for photos to protection money to prevent him from snatching Jessica.

Backtracking these calls, the FBI lab team lifted fingerprints from the public phones where the calls had been made. One of the prints matched those of Judge Wachtler secured by the Bureau.

Another call later in October warned that

Jessica would be kidnaped and, "Jessica is going to spend Thanksgiving with me," said the caller. The call came from Harrah's Club in Reno. Judge Wachtler was in Reno attending a convention and registered at Harrah's. A letter postmarked San Antonio, Texas with instructions for paying the ransom money on November 7 arrived.

A couple of weeks later, another phone call was traced back to a private club. Sol Wachtler was at that club at that time for a meeting. The next day, another call tracked back to a payphone in Roslyn, New York, "If you fuck up at all, I promise you it will cost you $200,000 to get your daughter back." FBI forensic experts went to Roslyn, found the pay phone that was used and lifted Wachtler's fingerprint from it.

Throughout all of this from the moment she discovered who it was, Joy had been beside herself. It was all so unnecessary. If Sol had a problem with their breakup, he should have told her and they could have worked it out in private. Now it was out of Joy's hands and the FBI wanted to be very sure they had Sol dead to rights and their agents were watching Wachtler night and day.

They followed him everywhere from home to court to political gatherings to Louisville, Kentucky from where he made another threatening call, a stop at a porno shop to buy some x-rated videotapes and playing cards. Then, he made a photocopy of one of the cards and sent it to Joy.

With coaching from the agents, Joy agreed to set up a payoff of the $20,000 at a location in midtown Manhattan. On the appointed date, November 7, agents followed Wachtler and staked out the payoff drop point.

On November 6, 1992, Wachtler had driven from his Long Island home to the state capital in Albany where he had given an interview to reporter Fred Dicker virtually announcing he was going to run for Governor of New York in 1994. That night he had been the featured speaker at a state bar association dinner.

The next morning Sol drove to Manhattan tailed by the FBI and with an FBI airplane overhead in case the ground crew lost him. Following instructions from the stalker, the FBI had secreted an envelope with the demanded $20,000 in it by the cellar stairs of the Shanley Laundry in midtown Manhattan.

On the way back from Albany, Wachtler pulled into a rest stop and made a phone call. Since it wasn't to Joy's rigged phone system, the FBI found out later that it was to the hairdresser's shop near where the $20,000 pay off was supposed to be hidden for pickup. He said he was David Samson and that he wanted somebody from the beauty salon to go over and pick up the envelope and hold it for him. There would be a big tip for whoever did it.

Sol then drove to his daughter's residence. Lauren Wachtler was also an attorney and, though married, always used her maiden name when in court or when carrying one of her father's briefcases with the official judicial seal on it. She was ambitious and close to Joy. Lauren and her father visited for a time before he left and went to the locality of the planned extortion payoff.

Wachtler drove to the area of the drop off in his state issued black Caprice. He parked the car, grabbed a brown envelope and a cowboy hat out of the truck and hailed a cab. With his cowboy hat on and pretending to be a Texan just in town, he gave the cabbie twenty bucks to deliver the manila envelope to Joy's place. This had in it a demand for more money.

Then, Wachtler did something unexpected. He didn't go to pick up the ransom money from the beauty parlor. Instead, he drove around aimlessly near the place where the ransom was hidden and then took off out of Manhattan, stopping first at a Mobil station at 90th and First street to gas up. Then, he drove across the East River on the Tri-Borough Bridge and out onto the Long Island Expressway.

The agents were in close pursuit and undecided what to do until they believed they saw him "destroying documents." They called in for instructions and U.S. Attorney Michael Chertoff directed them to arrest him.

When the agents identified themselves and arrested Wachtler, sitting on the front seat next to him was a device for altering the sound of voices.

The most incriminating aspect was none of the things the FBI had collected in the case up to that point. A good lawyer could have created reasonable doubt about the fingerprints and the voice altering device. But no lawyer can reason away guilt. The minute Wachtler was stopped and hauled in for questioning, he caved in and the admissions of his guilt gushed forth.

The case perplexed many people who knew Wachtler as a staid, straight-arrow jurist. Among those confounded was Norman Siegal, the Executive Director of the New York Civil Liberties Union, who knew Wachtler professionally,

You think you're in the Twilight Zone. There is nothing in the public life of Sol Wachtler that in any way would lead you to believe he could do any of these things.

Norman Siegal could ask how Sol Wachtler could do these things, but, do them he did.

Judge Grubin required Sol Wachtler to wear an electronic monitor bracelet and to pay for private security guards to see that he didn't leave his home in North Hills for anything but authorized visits to doctor, lawyers and the court.

On September 28, 1993, the gates of the medium-security Federal prison at Butner, North Carolina, closed behind Wachtler as he began his fifteen-month prison term. Today, he is back on the street.

Nineteen

Bob Krueger had once successfully run for Congress and, building on that, tried to run for the U.S. Senate against John Tower in 1984. To Texas-fy Krueger, who is a native but doesn't sound or act it, Bob Mann, his campaign press agent, had Krueger campaign around the state driving a semitrailer and announcing his arrival in every little town by blasting the air horn. It didn't work because it made him seem as out of place as Mary Poppins in the Chicken Ranch whorehouse.

To make it easier to cover the immense distances a candidate had to traverse in Texas, Krueger hired his own pilot and plane to ferry him and his wife Kathleen from appearance to appearance. It wasn't a fancy plane— a single-engine prop aircraft— and the pilot wasn't a fancy guy. Thomas Michael Humphrey seemed like a down-home, quiet, young man, with dark hair, pronounced eyebrows, and a boyish face akin to NBC anchorman Tom Brokaw's. To some people on the campaign, he did seem a

touch odd and had a deer-staring-into-the-
headlights look about him.

Two bad things came out of that ill-fated
campaign: First, Krueger lost narrowly. The
margin of loss was less than one-tenth of one
percent. And second, Tom Humphrey became obsessed with Kathleen. After the unsuccessful campaign, Humphrey started a
different kind of bid. It was to get Kathleen
for himself and, later when that failed, to kill
her. Kathleen described it:

> When we lost the Democratic primary
> in May 1984 . . . Tom Humphrey was
> devastated. We all were, of course, but
> he seemed to take the loss harder than
> even we did. Tom Humphrey was dev-
> astated. He was grief-stricken. I thought,
> he's taking this worse than Bob and I
> (sic) and Bob was the one who narrowly
> lost the election. His grief and despair
> [were] beyond normal.
>
> It was probably the best family feeling
> that he ever had in his life.

Usually, the staff of an unsuccessful political campaign dissolves quickly. The volun-
teers scatter back to their normal lives and
pick up the disrupted pieces or run off in
pursuit of another illusionary public office.

However, Tom Humphrey, because of his obsession with Kathleen, never left.

At first, Tom wouldn't accept the idea that the campaign was over and everybody had to go on to other things in life. He kept hanging around the Kruegers and told them that the year he had been with them was the most fulfilling time of his entire life. He professed his love for the Kruegers and all he could envision for the future was to stay close to them.

Bob and Kathleen were appreciative and let him come by the house and talked with him and let him share their lives a little longer because they felt sorry for Tom.

When Tom complained that he didn't know where he could find a place to live, the Kruegers agreed to rent Tom a house they owned adjacent to their own. From there he kept the Kruegers under careful watch and kept dropping by unannounced all the time.

"At times when I would come home from the grocery store," said Kathleen, "I would look across the street and I could see him peering between the blinds."

Finally, Bob Krueger sat Tom down for a serious talk about his situation and told him:

> Tom, you've got to move away. We just can't have you living here. You're our friend, but we just have to lead our own lives and you have to find your life. Tom, you need to get on with your life.

We're getting on with ours and we need
you to respect our privacy the same way
we'll respect yours.

Tom flipped. He didn't come over to the
Kruegers' house anymore, but he started
what would become an avalanche of telephone calls. Then, one day he came over
when Bob was gone, stepped inside, and
hugged Kathleen passionately. At that moment, she knew there was a problem:

And I knew there was something not
right. It was an instinctive knowing that
there was something not right. From that
point on I never let him inside the house.
His grip tightened and I realized he
might not let go. It wasn't sexual, but it
was eerie. I knew something wasn't right.
I thought, "What can I do to get out of
this situation?" So, I said, "Tom, would
you go out with me to check the mail?"

They walked outside, checked the mailbox
which Kathleen knew would be empty because it was too early for the mail, and she
turned to him as they stood on the street and
said "goodbye." Fortunately, he simply stood
there doing nothing while she walked back
into the house and locked the door.

From that moment on, Kathleen and Bob
Krueger and, years later, their two young

daughters, Mariana and Sarah became prisoners in their own home. They didn't dare answer the door or go outside except directly to their cars to leave the premises. They were fearful that Humphrey would be lurking somewhere out there and, as time went on, he might try to harm them even after Bob Krueger forced Tom to move out of the house they had let him use.

The Kruegers kept their blinds and drapes closed and were constantly peering out to check that Tom wasn't somewhere nearby. When the doorbell rang, they would peek out from a vantage point where they could see the front door without being seen before deciding whether or not to answer the door. Tom came to the door from time to time and repeatedly rang the bell. Kathleen began to time his ringing and it would last fifteen to twenty minutes at a time, but she refused to answer the door.

For the next nine years Tom kept writing and calling and leaving forty and fifty messages on their answering machine every day. Even when he got a job in California, he continued to call at all hours of the day and night:

I left something in your mailbox. You can do with it whatever you want, but I just want you to know that if I wanted to wipe you out, you would be dead right now. You are going to die.

Or, another message:

I'll just keep coming back again and
again and again and again. I know I'm
right. I just love you so much, goddamn
it! I don't know how to hide it. I can't.
I drink you in and I am in ecstasy.
KATHLEE-EE-EE-E-N!

They could hear the longing and the pain in
his voice as he called out her name like a lost
soul beseeching the gods to relieve his agony.

Finally, Kathleen lost her patience with this
intolerable situation. One day in May of
1985, she snatched up the telephone and
screamed into the receiver, "Leave us alone!"

There was dead silence from the other end
of the line, and Kathleen regained her com-
posure, returning to her normal tone but still
with an edge on it. "I think you enjoy this,"
she said to her tormentor and he quietly replied, "You're right. I do."

She hung up determined to do something
to stop the torture; first, Bob tried to reason
with Tom to no avail. The Kruegers contacted and spoke with Humphrey's parents in
the hope that they might help. They refused
to cooperate and maintained that the
Kruegers were making up stories about their
son and they wanted nothing to do with it.

* * *

One of the problems facing the Kruegers was that Bob was a congressman and, later, U.S. Ambassador-at-Large to Mexico. It was essential that his phone number be listed so people with legitimate business could reach him.

When the calls from California started coming they went to the police who said there was nothing they could do. They went to the FBI and used every legal and government connection Bob had. They figured, since the calls were coming from across state lines, that made Humphrey's calls a federal offense, but Bob and Kathleen were wrong. There was nothing the FBI could do either.

Kathleen explained what every law-enforcement agency told them, "We're sorry, but we can't do anything until he tries to physically hurt you."

Bob became incredibly frustrated:

Society has a right to be protected against people like this. I served as a U.S. congressman and ambassador. I knew people in so-called positions of power. And if we suffer that way, how do other people suffer?

So, the calls kept coming and coming, dozens and dozens of times a day.

* * *

When Kathleen got pregnant in 1987, she and Bob abandoned easy access by clients or constituents and unlisted their home phone number so that Kathleen could get a respite from Humphrey's telephone harassment at their home. Humphrey switched to calling Bob's office number, which had an answering machine on it.

As Bob described it, his business answering machine had a one-hour tape, and every morning when he came to work the tape was filled with messages from Tom Humphrey. Bob's machine cut the caller off after thirty seconds. Tom had to redial Bob's office number 120 times a night to leave his 120 thirty-second messages. Even if Tom had a redial feature on his phone, it still took determination to leave 120 messages every night.

It was worth it to Tom because he was getting his messages through to Bob and Kathleen, who were listening to those 120 messages in thirty-second spurts. Tom's campaign was working at least to the extent that he was not being ignored and what he was saying was getting into the brains of the Kruegers. They continued to listen, hoping for something that would help them make Tom stop and to keep alert to his plans and any possible threatening moves he might make:

You can have me arrested, but you're going to die. I'll watch you die. So, you'd better be scared of that, you. So, you better get me before I get you.

As time went on, Tom became more and more abusive and more threatening. Kathleen remembers, "The first specific death threat came when I was pregnant for the first time with my first child. I believed that I would give birth as a widow."

That was at Christmas time in 1987:

I'm going to kill you. I'm going to kill you. I'm going to kill you. I've hired a killer to put a .22 caliber to your head while you lie sleeping next to your wife. You won't be much of an ambassador with a hole in your head.

The irritation of listening to his hundreds of messages over and over again, week after week, finally paid off. There was now a specific, illegal threat to murder Bob and, since it was made on a phone call from California to Texas and crossed state lines, the federal authorities could be brought into the Kruegers' battle for peace and protection.

The FBI agreed with Krueger's assessment and wanted to help in any way it legally could. The agency dispatched a special agent to Humphrey's California home to arrest Tom and settle the matter. When the FBI showed up, Tom was gone.

The immediate findings that the FBI shared with Kathleen and Bob was that Tom had left California and was on his way back to Texas to carry out his threat to murder Bob. The Feds urged the Kruegers to get out of their house immediately. It didn't take much urging. They were scared out of their minds and hastily packed a few things and were gone. Tom had triumphed again. He had driven them out of their own home.

Going into hiding until the FBI stopped their stalker, was also a ploy to trap Tom. The Kruegers went to Kathleen's parents' ranch in Bandera which, if Tom knew as much about them as they thought he did, he'd be aware of. It wouldn't take a genius to figure out that running home to mom and dad would be a logical option if the Kruegers fled their own home.

Despite this flaw, it worked out successfully. Bob had his office phone put on call-forwarding to the Bandera ranch. The FBI had given them a telephone tape recorder so they could make a record of incoming calls. However, electronic wizardry couldn't do what Bob and Kathleen did by themselves in catching Tom Humphrey.

Bob said he wanted to personally answer all the calls at the Bandera place knowing that sooner or later Tom would call the office, the call would be forwarded, and contact would be made. It happened sooner rather than later. The third forwarded call was Tom.

Bob began talking carefully with Tom who said he wanted to talk with Kathleen. Bob told Tom that Kathleen couldn't come to the phone because she was "at home," letting Tom think he had called Krueger's office. Bob said he would have Kathleen call Tom back and asked for his telephone number.

Obsession-blinded Tom instantly gave Bob the telephone number for Kathleen to call and Bob quietly ended the conversation. Moments later, Krueger was giving the number to the FBI and within hours they had arrested Tom at a hotel in California.

That should have ended the Kruegers' cruel experience with obsessed stalker, but it didn't work.

In May of 1989, Thomas Michael Humphrey pled guilty in federal court to interstate extortion and death threats. A few weeks later on July 19, he was sentenced to federal prison for twelve-months with three years' probation after that.

Temporarily, Kathleen was elated, but later she became bitter, "I felt such relief. I felt that this would be the end of it. That was almost five years ago and it wasn't the end of it."

Driving offenses can mean longer jail terms, and, many prisoners don't have to

serve out the full terms of their sentence.
Tom was no different. He was put into the
slammer on July 19 and was back on the
street three days after Christmas after serving
about five months.

Whatever relief the Kruegers felt in July of
1989, they were robbed of by early 1990. Tom
was back on the phone with the death threats
just about the time Kathleen was due with
their second child, Sarah.

The new pattern of harassment made it
clear that Tom knew he would be punished
for his stalking Kathleen, but he was willing
to undergo that since he was winning the battle in many ways. Just as Hinckley said of
Jodie Foster for whom he stalked and shot
Ronald Reagan, the stalker had succeeded in
one of his goals. He had become an unfor-
gettable part of his victim's life in spite of
everything the victim did to block him out.

As soon as they documented Humphrey's
new threats, the Kruegers were able to have
him arrested again and sent back to prison.
This time for six months.

A psychologist might suggest that stalkers
who are punished accept their punishment
as a form of martyrdom to their love, to their
obsession, and as proof of what they are willing to endure to show their devotion. History
is loaded with examples of people who invite

persecution and punishment for their devotion as a sacred offering and certification of their love.

The second jail term didn't do any more good than the first one, and Tom continued his threats and stalking until he was arrested and jailed for a third time in October of 1991. He was put away this time until the end of July 1993.

The main point of this case is that the authorities were helpless to stop Tom until he made illegal threats. If he hadn't threatened to kill Bob, Tom could have gone on forever with his 120 phone calls a night and letters and stalking.

It was this personal experience that got Bob Krueger appointed a U.S. senator for a few months in 1993, to sponsor federal anti-stalking legislation. Senator Lloyd Bentsen had been made Secretary of the Treasury, and Gov. Ann Richards appointed Krueger to fill the vacant seat.

Twenty

Given that many stalkers are emotionally sick and some are homicidal, are we doing everything we can to keep them under control?

One of the joys of living in our society is that it is free and open, and one of the great menaces of living in our society is that it is free and open.

We are confused trying to figure out what are the limits of freedom. We are entitled to freedom of speech, but as Justice Oliver Wendell Holmes, Jr., said in 1919, that doesn't give us the right to shout "fire" in a crowded theater. The Supreme Court also recognizes the concept of "fighting words." These are words that are so offensive, so insulting, so abrasive that they can justify a physical attack. Therefore, there is a limit to freedom of speech as there is on other Constitutional rights.

For example, it's your Constitutional right to bear arms, but few would quarrel with the prohibition of private parties owning an A-bomb. Others believe in the rights of a free press, but that right is often in conflict with the accused's right to trial by an impartial jury.

Our leaders and philosophers say that we have a Constitutional right to privacy, but, the business entrepreneurs of the country trample that assumption into the mud.

Businesses have wide access to information about everybody including celebrities. The same access is accorded to private detectives, department stores, credit card companies, oil companies, or to anybody willing to pay a fee to find out information about you including your social security number, your address, your phone number, etc.

Privacy has fallen victim to the computer age. Information about everything we do, from buying a car to making a phone call, is fed into hundreds of databases owned by credit bureaus, the government, banks, insurance companies and direct marketing companies. These data banks send out the information to information sellers across the country, who make it available to anyone who is on-line.

Information is collected about everybody by medical bureaus; by stores from whom you buy things; by people running 800 and 900 numbers; and by the government itself. There are at least 178 Federal government agencies that keep two thousand data banks of information on all of us including celebrities. Add to that hundreds more state and local agencies that do the same thing.

For example, for a few dollars stalkers were easily able to get Vanna White's home telephone number and Rebecca Schaeffer's home address. One of them harassed Vanna for years and the other murdered Rebecca.

Even though your Social Security number, which is the basic code number for getting private information, is supposed to be kept confidential, many agencies use it as an identity number. The State of Virginia, for example, uses it as your driver's license number.

There are laws such as the Financial Privacy Act of 1978 that are supposed to protect you from people pawing through your bank records, but most of them— including the Financial Privacy Act of 1978— are basically worthless.

All the periodic hand-wringing about privacy invasion is good for the occasional wishy-washy law with the brave title and for a few minutes on *60 Minutes* or *20/20*, but nothing serious is done. Beyond that, nothing serious will be done because the American people haven't really demanded it.

One reason they haven't is their insatiable curiosity about celebrities. They want privacy for themselves and their families only. Tabloids sell well because they reveal the private lives of screen idols.

"Idol worship is a mild drug for most people, but it turns to poison in others," says Gavin de Becker. "Idolatry is normal in America."

Dr. Park Dietz and a group of experts studied stalkers of Hollywood stars and members of Congress for the U.S. Justice Department in which they analyzed threats and crank mail sent over a three-year period. The study revealed that there are about 150,000 stalkers out there today. It says that "they are a deadly new breed of killer: violent, mentally ill individuals who choose public figures as targets."

Dietz believes, "there are several reasons for that large a number. Today, we have a lot of mentally ill people who are no longer supervised."

This has an ironic twist to it as I have mentioned before because politicians have tried to look good by cutting budgets for health care and have ended up releasing the mentally disturbed, who threaten those same politicians.

Inadvertently, the politicians have created their own stalkers, which may please some people, but some of those stalkers are endangering innocent celebrities, too.

According to Jim Cruse, who was a *National Enquirer* reporter for three years before he was fired for trying to write a book about the tabloid, *Enquirer* reporters have sold the addresses and phone numbers of stars to fans and, in some cases, stalkers. When Olympic diver Greg Louganis was confronted by a mentally ill stalker, they found out that the man had gotten Louganis's address from a *National Enquirer* reporter for a bribe.

The most interesting thing about the study Dietz helped to make for the U.S. Justice Department, which was released in the autumn of 1989, was that he and his fellow researchers developed a technique that allows them to figure out when the critical point has been reached with a stalker— when the stalker will try to make physical contact with his victim and take action.

In his book, *Intimate Strangers*, Richard Schickel argues that the fault lies with television and the media that switches off reality in our heads and lets us fantasize about relationships with celebrities and public figures.

He draws an analogy to the plot of the movie *King of Comedy*, in which the character Rupert Pupkin is the stalking, fantasizing, kidnapping, wanna-be comic. With television turning all well-known people into "intimate strangers" the devil's work begins when we perceive that our TV-created friendships turn to rejection and our unrequited love turns to revenge.

Security expert de Becker believes the motivation of the star stalker is envy. In his eyes the first star stalker was Alexander Ivanovich

Dorogokupetz who stood up at a Frank Sinatra concert in New York and threw an egg
to protest Sinatra's wealth and success. He
doesn't put much faith in interviewing stalkers themselves, "The worst place to look for
insight into a celebrity stalker is the celebrity
stalker himself. He'll tell you anything. That
God made him do it. That the devil told him
to do it. That a book told him to do it. That
an animal told him to do it. In nearly every
case, the celebrity stalker simply wants the
attention for once."

Not only are television and movies blamed
for inciting stalkers, but so are books. In a
Frontline documentary (February 9, 1988)
about Mark David Chapman, the blame rests
on a book popular with many generations
over the years, *The Catcher in the Rye*.

According to Chapman's views on this
show, he became obsessed with J.D. Salinger's story which revolved around a teenage
character named Holden Caulfield, who has
the adolescent insight to reject the phoniness
and the sour hypocrisy of the adults who
muck up the world and accept, in its stead,
the innocence and honor of the young.

To Chapman, Lennon had turned away
from the purity of childhood innocence,
abandoned pursuit of noble ideals, and had
become "one of the biggest phonies of our
time." On this television analysis of him,
Chapman was described as:

A big druggie and Beatles fan during his high school days in a suburb near Atlanta who later became a born-again Christian who loved to work with children as a camp counselor. Often sullen, withdrawn, and depressed, he moved to Hawaii in the late seventies and, after an unsuccessful suicide attempt, got married. After reading a book by Lennon, Chapman decided he was going to kill him.

Chapman vacillated between horror at his own act of violence and perverse pride in what he had done because, "the Beatles changed the world as we know it, and I changed them. It's the last nail in the coffin of the sixties and I am the 'Catcher in the Rye' of this generation."

This TV program pinned the blame for the tragedy on Chapman, who was a celebrity stalker who did what he did knowingly. Still, early in the program, the crime was blamed on the book as the narrator intoned, "The novel became Chapman's script for murder and its central character, Holden Caulfield, became Chapman's vehicle for carrying out the act."

Dr. Park Dietz appeared on the program and contradicted that contention and blamed television instead, which he believes is the root of antisocial behavior.

That, of course, opened up a whole issue with champions on all political spectrums claiming television is the cause of society's ills. Meanwhile, others contend that the problem is not *on* television but *in* people's minds with hundreds of millions of people seeing things on TV, but only a few copying them.

Mankind has been obsessed with the worship of idols from the beginning of time. Our time is no different from any other except now it's covered on *60 Minutes*.

Societal critics like to point out how modern stalking has become.

Just as computers, E-mail, and Internet are becoming a part of human life, so must stalking expect to become computerized and where more appropriately than in the life of the richest computer whiz in the world, Bill Gates, the founder and chief honcho of Microsoft.

Gates prides himself on his accessibility through E-mail, which is private and which he claims to read religiously.

The name Redmond Rose is the computer moniker for Joan L. Brewer, divorced mother of three, who has been employed at two different divisions of Microsoft since 1989 and fired from each of them; was interviewed and rejected by a third; and worked as a temp at a fourth and was fired from that. There is no doubt that Ms. Brewer is intelligent and well educated with a degree in computer systems from the Oregon Institute of Technology with a minor in laser electro-optics, but she has been deemed unsuitable for employment at Microsoft because "she is too technical and her telephone calls are too long," according to one assessment.

Ms. Brewer struck back initially by writing E-mail to Bill Gates, complaining about her treatment, sexual harassment, and hiring discrimination. She filed a complaint with the Equal Employment Opportunity Commission that was dismissed and a sexual harassment lawsuit that was also summarily dismissed.

However, in time, the E-mail turned mean with Brewer charging all sorts of dark motivations to Gates's isolated lifestyle and behavior. She also likened Gates to fairy-tale characters such as Peter Pan or Pinocchio in the more than one hundred letters she has E-mailed to him.

From harassment and discrimination complaints to psychological analysis and fairy tales, the E-mail barrage turned from mean ridicule to threats.

Ms. Brewer had some more dramatic ideas of communicating her points including, according to Bill Gates, threats to drive a car through the entrance of Microsoft and to blow the place up.

This left Mr. Gates with a pain in his head

and he turned it over to the attorneys who went to court. Shaking his head, the judge issued a restraining order to keep Ms. Brewer from sending Mr. Gates any more E-mail and to keep her from getting close to the compugenius. That was January 1991 and was lifted a year later. She has started the E-mail again, although a bit more restrained this time.

Twenty-one

When things go wrong in society, many in power immediately react by wanting to pass a law as if that was all that was required. Passing laws is what legislators, lawyers, and social elitists think is the magic elixir, but for ordinary people too often laws are meaningless.

The inability of law enforcement to do much about stalkers was a major motivation behind the passage of antistalker laws. In a 1989 seminar on celebrity protection, Capt. Robert Martin of the Los Angeles Police Department spoke of the situation the police faced at that time:

> I hate to tell you, but if we get a letter of threat we're just mildly interested. No crime has been committed, no reports are generated. We don't do anything with it. You call up and say, "Some screwball's in my neighborhood." We say, "Call us when he does something." I know that's not what you want to hear. But that's the way it is.

FBI agent Kenneth Jacobson echoed Captain Martin's grim reality for the celebrity managers and agents who attended that seminar:

I cannot guarantee you immediate action. If you call in a panic and say somebody is outside your client's house right now, you've called the wrong agency. If we conduct an investigation, are fortunate enough to identify the individual who's doing the threats and are able to amass a case that is prosecutable under the statutes, I still can't guarantee it will be prosecuted.

In Los Angeles, for example, you are dealing with limited resources and a grossly understaffed U.S. Attorney's Office. We have probably the biggest drug problem in the United States right now. We have one of the biggest bank-failure problems. We have rampant white-collar crime. The threat may be important to you, but it's not going to be one of the priorities of the U.S. Attorney's Office.

Pulitzer Prize-winning *Washington Post* reporter George Learner, Jr., wrote about a young woman named Kristin who was studying art at Tufts University and who began dating Michael Cartier in Boston. He was a bouncer at a local nightclub when their romance began in January 1992.

After a few months, he began playing bouncer with her, knocking her around when she didn't do what he wanted. She broke off their relationship and told him to take a long hike. He refused. He began stalking her.

He followed her around, often showing up at the liquor store where she worked and constantly calling her on the phone. She went from annoyance to irritation to terror in a short time, and knowing he was on probation, she complained to his probation officer. It was only then that she found out why he was on probation. With a pair of scissors, he had gone after a previous girlfriend who had dumped him.

Kristin followed the system and the system responded by doing the paperwork to order Cartier to stay away from her. She got two restraining orders from the courts, but these merely kept Cartier two hundred feet away from her. At this point, the overburdened system stalled out on her, and the paperwork didn't go forward so that an arrest warrant would be issued to haul this scissors-wielding guy out of Kristin's life.

While she was waiting for the system to do something, Cartier didn't wait and he did something. Angry at her for trying to get him arrested, he lost it. On May 30 he tracked her down Commonwealth Avenue near where she worked and trapped her, brutalized her and then shot her dead. The system can't reach him for what he did to Kristin, because seconds later he, turned the gun on himself. Now they are both dead while the system blunders on as best it can.

George Learner traced this incident carefully and in detail to illustrate how the classic clumsy bureaucracy failed to protect the victim of a stalker. Learner won a Pulitzer Prize for this story, but he won it with a heavy heart. Kristin was his daughter.

We now have antistalking laws in forty-eight states and they are a mess. There are at least three major problems with antistalker laws.

First, they try to forbid behavior that is acceptable at some times by some people. Some antistalking laws are so broadly drawn or so vague that they could apply to anyone in town. For example, they could apply to a legitimate news reporter covering a political official.

In other cases, they are so narrowly drawn that they apply to nobody in town.

If a man courts a woman, he might violate the state's stalking laws even though she enjoys and wants the attention. On the other hand, if he does it too arduously in the face of her rejection and she doesn't enjoy it and doesn't want the attention, it also violates the stalking laws. Who interprets? Who decides?

Joan Zorza, an attorney with the National Center of Women and Family Law, says that, "One of the problems with the laws is that they're not going to cover many victims that need protection."

The vague language in some laws says things like a person is guilty if they cause another person "reasonable" fear of being attacked or killed. So who decides what is "reasonable"? Zorza notes, "What might not be terrifying to a reasonable man is terrifying to a reasonable woman."

In the case of ice-skater Katarina Witt, her stalker was arrested, tried, and put away for a time. In the case of Caroline Witt, in the Greater Chicago area, it didn't work out that way. Her former boyfriend sent flowers and notes and called over and over again. Finally, he ran her down with his car and killed her.

Caroline had tried to get police protection, but the police said her case didn't meet the standards set by Illinois's tough antistalking law. In the same Chicago area, Kimberly Globis's case did meet those standards and she did get court orders requiring the man stalking her to stay away. It didn't mean a damn to her ex-boyfriend. Two days after Witt was run down, Leslie Peace sought out Kimberly and shot her dead in front of her two children.

The confusion in antistalking laws may someday be cleared up. The National Conference of State Legislature, the American Bar Association, and the National Criminal Justice Association are all working on their versions of a model antistalking law, but it will take a long time for it to get accepted and for the state legislatures in every state to modify what they now have.

This raises point two. Laws are designed to restrain those people sane enough to understand what they mean and what the consequences are for disobeying them. Most rational people don't break the law because they don't want to pay the penalty. But, with the emotionally challenged and deranged stalker, the law doesn't mean a thing. We saw that with Tom Humphrey's stalking of the Kruegers. Tom didn't care how many times they put him in jail, he was going to continue to stalk the Kruegers whenever he was out.

The law only works in the outside world if it works inside the head of the stalker. Stanton Samenow, Virginia clinical psychologist and author of *Inside The Criminal Mind*, says that "many have disturbed self-images in which they see themselves as irresistible or complete zeros. [Ralph Nau is an example of the former and Mark David Chapman of the latter.] When they are rejected, they resort to intimidation in a desperate attempt to regain self-esteem. The threat of prison may deter some of them, but for others it's like putting fuel on a fire."

Finally, the law may be fine, but police are already overburdened with laws to enforce and they can't really respond to threats easily. Lack of manpower often makes them limit their responses to actual physical attacks. This was the case, for example, with the Theresa Saldana situation. Beyond that, stalker victims often are too sympathetic to their stalker or too afraid of him or her to follow through with making charges and testifying.

CNN's Catherine Crier on her program *Crier & Company* tried to see if the newly in-vogue antistalker laws being considered around the country will do any good. In imitation of California's landmark antistalker law, forty-eight states have now passed such laws against willful, malicious, and repeated harassing of another person with sentences ranging from thirty days up to seven years.

Most of these have been passed as the result of a notorious stalking case. In California it was the Rebecca Schaeffer murder by stalker Robert Bardo; in New York, the Amy Fisher-Mary Jo Buttafuoco case; and, in Connecticut, the David Letterman incidents.

A federal antistalker law was considered under pressure from the former senator from Texas, Robert Krueger, whose wife has been a stalker victim for almost a decade.

Here's Catherine Crier's introduction, "Stalkers, known and unknown, incite terror with an insidious presence that pervades their victims' lives. In most states, there's little police can do to stop it."

Then, she turned to her three guests on the subject, Greta Van Susteren, a Washington, D.C., trial lawyer; Cheryl Ward, Assistant City Attorney for Los Angeles and Chairwoman of the Los Angeles County Domestic Violence Council; and Alan Begner, a First Amendment attorney. Not surprisingly, they all had different views about antistalking laws.

Van Susteren favored such laws, not just because she was an attorney, but because she had the personal experience of being a stalking victim herself.

* * *

The California Stalker Law, which has not been fully tested in the courts yet and cannot be considered solid until it is, concerns many people who care about civil rights for everyone.

Basically, it creates a new kind of crime. It makes it a criminal act to merely be somewhere that other people are allowed to be. It tries to narrow the crime by requiring the "criminal" to do it twice. Even so, think about how wide such a law is. It makes your merely being present twice in the same place near the same person a criminal act.

For example, if you wait at the same bus stop as someone else and that makes the other person nervous or apprehensive, you could go to jail in California if you spoke or acted in a way the other person thought threatening. This law was passed in 1990 as a result of celebrity stalkings and the Rebecca Schaeffer murder.

The issue is twofold. Is such a law Constitutional and does it do any good? Would it have prevented the ex-mailman from invading the Southern California post office in search of the woman with whom he was obsessed and killing several innocent people in the process? Would it have prevented the Upstate New York fifty-nine-year-old rejected lover from killing all those people with bombs? Would it, in fact, have saved Rebecca Schaeffer from being murdered?

The answer in all cases is no. Historically it is proven that laws do not deter emotionally obsessed and determined people. These laws are like the security gates in apartment complexes which really only keep out cars— not people on foot— or the sign-in registers in office buildings. The killer comes in, signs a phony name, and he's on the elevator up to where you are.

Do these determined people care about antistalker laws? Not for a second.

Would the California law have worked to protect Greta Van Susteren? Even she admitted it wouldn't:

> The California law does require something more. It does require threats. And the man who followed me never threatened. He was just always there and his conduct— and I researched it very extensively— was constitutional. It was just frankly annoying.
>
> The real problem here, though, is not the annoying conduct of having him there all the time. It's a question of what do we do about the potential for danger. And, in my situation, there was no way that I could be sure and frankly, that's true in every situation. You don't know if someone's going to be dangerous.
>
> We have to wait till someone makes that

overt act, whether it's a threat or an assault, and then we need to move swiftly. The criminal justice system just does not move swiftly, though.

On the Crier program, Ms. Ward underscored the stupidity of the law in *preventing* crimes by stalkers:

> The restraining order is good for individuals who understand it and decide they're going to comply with it. That makes the restraining order good.

In other words, the antistalking order has to be enforced by the stalker himself or herself for it to work!

Ms. Ward continued:

> For a number of these individuals, however, who we refer to as stalkers, they have some sort of mental problem which makes it difficult for them to understand the realities and, of course, that restraining order wouldn't be very effective toward them.

Alan Begner on the same program understood the realities, namely, antistalking laws might make things worse:

> It seems to me that stalkers are nuts. They are uncontrollable by the system,

no matter what you have, be it a stalker law or criminal laws that are already in place. Because the stalker laws create misdemeanors out of these things, and they'll be out of jail [in a short time] and are likely to be the most determined people of all within the system.

Van Susteren argued that stalkers were already failed by the mental health system and so that giving them mental consulting was useless and the criminal system was the only answer. Yet, in the next breath, she admitted that the criminal justice system was also useless against a stalker such as the one who dogged her for eight years of her life:

I think we have to wait for an actual event [a threat or violent act by the stalker], because we can't just go around arresting people whose presence we don't like. The man who followed me was an enormous pest. It was incredible, the way he was obsessed with me, but he didn't violate any law.

Attorney Alan Begner regretfully agreed:

Unfortunately, I have no good recommendations for victims. Stalkers are hardcore and dedicated people [particularly those in pursuit of celebrities, public figures and stars]. There is nothing, really, you can do to them that will make them want to stop. In my view, and unfortunately, in weighing the rights of the stalkers and the rights of victims, I think you have to wait until there is the threat and then have them arrested for the assault, for the threat.

Celebrities are now painfully aware of the dangers of stalkers. They are now demanding that production companies provide them with adequate protection while working.

The well-known burglar alarm system company ADT Security Systems has now entered the field of personal protection against criminals and, particularly, stalkers. It offers a pendant with a panic button that can be pushed if the wearer is in danger. This transmits a low-power radio signal to a nearby receiver in the wearer's home and that dials the telephone with a recording to call the police.

Obviously, this system is limited to those wearing it around and near their home, and some stalkers, wise to the system, have disconnected home telephones to disable it.

Another device currently being used to protect entertainment celebrities is a new computer program known as the Threat Data Tracking System. Run by Noel Koch, president of International Security Management, threatening letters, phone calls, and photographs are fed into the system to analyze their characteristics and determine whether or not the stalkers are likely to commit a direct, dangerous act against the star. "Once we get a line on these people, we hope to be able to predict what will trigger them to commit violent actions. Then, we can develop a more effective intervention strategy whether that means protecting the victim or restraining the stalker."

Koch says that the celebrity stalker is the one who fabricates love relationships with public figures who don't even know them.

Beth Finkelstein, a senior analyst at ISM, says the celebrity stalker is the most difficult to spot initially:

> The first letters or phone calls received by a victim might seem relatively innocuous and often don't get noted right away. Only after letters and phone calls increase in length and volume do people finally take action, by which time valuable data has been lost.
>
> Also, letters or phone calls may be received by several members of a celebrity's entourage instead of the celebrities themselves making it more difficult to coordinate information and access the level of danger posed by a potential stalker.

* * *

There are those who think the solution to everything is a new law. But, cynics like Phil Gutis of the American Civil Liberties Union don't agree. Says Gutis:

> Antistalking laws are a popular thing to do. Legislators don't have to spend any money and a politician can say, "I'm so concerned about women, I'm passing this law," they look like heroes, but in the meantime they have done nothing.
>
> Women have been complaining to the police [for years]; they just haven't gotten any attention. To deal with the problem effectively, we've got to change attitudes in the criminal justice system and add some enforcement dollars.

The courts must be uniform in what sentences they hand out for violations of antistalking laws, which are often only misdemeanors and put the stalker back on the street in relatively short time.

The problem of stalkers may never be completely solved, but it can be lessened by a combination of awareness and legislation.

ORDINARY LIVES DESTROYED BY EXTRAORDINARY HORROR.
FACTS MORE DANGEROUS THAN FICTION.
CAPTURE A PINNACLE TRUE CRIME . . . IF YOU DARE.

INFORMATIVE —
COMPELLING —
SCINTILLATING —
NON-FICTION FROM PINNACLE TELLS THE TRUTH!

BORN TOO SOON (751, $4.50)
by Elizabeth Mehren
This is the poignant story of Elizabeth's daughter Emily's premature birth. As the parents of one of the 275,000 babies born prematurely each year in this country, she and her husband were plunged into the world of the Neonatal Intensive Care unit. With stunning candor, Elizabeth Mehren relates her gripping story of unshakable faith and hope — and of courage that comes in tiny little packages.

THE PROSTATE PROBLEM (745, $4.50)
by Chet Cunningham
An essential, easy-to-use guide to the treatment and prevention of the illness that's in the headlines. This book explains in clear, practical terms all the facts. Complete with a glossary of medical terms, and a comprehensive list of health organizations and support groups, this illustrated handbook will help men combat prostate disorder and lead longer, healthier lives.

THE ACADEMY AWARDS HANDBOOK (887, $4.50)
An interesting and easy-to-use guide for movie fans everywhere, the book features a year-to-year listing of all the Oscar nominations in every category, all the winners, an expert analysis of who wins and why, a complete index to get information quickly, and even a 99% foolproof method to pick this year's winners!

WHAT WAS HOT (894, $4.50)
by Julian Biddle
Journey through 40 years of the trends and fads, famous and infamous figures, and momentous milestones in American history. From hoola hoops to rap music, greasers to yuppies, Elvis to Madonna — it's all here, trivia for all ages. An entertaining and evocative overview of the milestones in America from the 1950's to the 1990's!

Available wherever paperbacks are sold, or order direct from the Publisher. Send cover price plus 50¢ per copy for mailing and handling to Penguin USA, P.O. Box 999, c/o Dept. 17109, Bergenfield, NJ 07621. Residents of New York and Tennessee must include sales tax. DO NOT SEND CASH.